MULTICULTURAL SCENES FOR YOUNG ACTORS

CRAIG SLAIGHT is the director of the Young Conservatory at the American Conservatory Theater in San Francisco. Prior to joining A.C.T., Mr. Slaight was head of the acting and directing program at the Los Angeles County High School for the Arts. He also served on the theater faculty at the Interlochen Center for the Arts. In addition to his commitment to developing and training young actors, Mr. Slaight spent ten years in Los Angeles as a professional director. He currently serves as a consultant to the Educational Theatre Association and is a member of the Theater Panel for ARTS, sponsored by the National Foundation for Advancement in the Arts. He is co-editor (with Jack Sharrar) of *Great Scenes for Young Actors from the Stage*, *Great Monologues for Young Actors*, *Great Scenes and Monologues For Children*, and *New Plays from A.C.T.'s Young Conservatory*.

JACK SHARRAR is Registrar and Director of Graduate Studies for the American Conservatory Theater, where he also teaches acting, directing, and voice. Mr. Sharrar is a graduate of the University of Michigan, and holds a Ph.D. in theater history and dramatic literature from the University of Utah. He is author of *Avery Hopwood, His Life and Plays*; contributor to Oxford University Press's *The American National Biography*, and co-author (with Craig Slaight) of *Great Scenes for Young Actors from the Stage*, *Great Monologues for Young Actors*, which the New York Public Library recognized as one of the Best Books for the Teenage 1993, and *Great Scenes and Monologues For Children*.

Smith and Kraus *Books For Actors*

THE MONOLOGUE SERIES

The Best Men's / Women's Stage Monologues of 1992
The Best Men's / Women's Stage Monologues of 1991
The Best Men's / Women's Stage Monologues of 1990
One Hundred Men's / Women's Stage Monologues from the 1980's
2 Minutes and Under: Character Monologues for Actors
Street Talk: Character Monologues for Actors
Uptown: Character Monologues for Actors
Monologues from Contemporary Literature: Volume I
Monologues from Classic Plays
100 Great Monologues from the Renaissance Theatre
100 Great Monologues from the Neo-Classical Theatre
100 Great Monologues from the 19th C. Romantic and Realistic Theatres

FESTIVAL MONOLOGUE SERIES

The Great Monologues from the Humana Festival
The Great Monologues from the EST Marathon
The Great Monologues from the Women's Project
The Great Monologues from the Mark Taper Forum

YOUNG ACTORS SERIES

Great Scenes and Monologues for Children
New Plays from A.C.T.'s Young Conservatory
Great Scenes for Young Actors from the Stage
Great Monologues for Young Actors
Multicultural Monologues for Young Actors
Multicultural Scenes for Young Actors

SCENE STUDY SERIES

Scenes From Classic Plays 468 B.C. to 1960 A.D.
The Best Stage Scenes of 1993
The Best Stage Scenes of 1992
The Best Stage Scenes for Men / Women from the 1980's

CONTEMPORARY PLAYWRIGHTS SERIES

Romulus Linney: 17 Short Plays
Eric Overmyer: Collected Plays
Lanford Wilson: 21 Short Plays
William Mastrosimone: Collected Plays
Horton Foote: 4 New Plays
Israel Horovitz: 16 Short Plays
Terrence McNally: 15 Short Plays
Humana Festival '93: The Complete Plays
Humana Festival '94: The Complete Plays
Women Playwrights: The Best Plays of 1992
Women Playwrights: The Best Plays of 1993

GREAT TRANSLATION FOR ACTORS SERIES

The Wood Demon by Anton Chekhov

CAREER DEVELOPMENT SERIES

The Camera Smart Actor
The Sanford Meisner Approach
The Actor's Chekhov
Kiss and Tell: Restoration Scenes, Monologues, & History
Cold Readings: Some Do's and Don'ts for Actors at Auditions

If you require prepublication information about upcoming Smith and Kraus books, you may receive our semi-annual catalogue, free of charge, by sending your name and address to *Smith and Kraus Catalogue, P.O. Box 127, One Main Street, Lyme, NH 03768. Or call us at (800) 895-4331, fax (603) 795-4427.*

MULTICULTURAL SCENES FOR YOUNG ACTORS

Craig Slaight and Jack Sharrar, Editors

The Young Actors Series

SK

A Smith and Kraus Book

A Smith and Kraus Book
Published by Smith and Kraus, Inc.
One Main Street, Lyme, NH 03768
603.795.4331

Cover and Text Design By Julia Hill
Original Cover Art: *Fish II* © by Irene Kelly from the collection of Marisa and Eric Kraus
Manufactured in the United States of America

First Edition: April 1995
10 9 8 7 6 5 4 3 2 1

Library of Congress Cataloging-in-Publication Data
Multicultural scenes for young actors / Craig Slaight and Jack Sharrar, editors. --1st ed.
      p. cm. -- (The Young actors series)
      ISBN 1-880399-48-2

CURR
PN
2080
M87
1995

      1. Acting. 2. Drama--Collections. 3. Multiculturalism. [1. Acting. 2. Plays.]
      I. Slaight, Craig, 1951- . II. Sharrar, Jack F., 1949- . III. Series.

      PN2080.M87   1994
      808.82'45--dc20   94-44187
                                                                    CIP
                                                                          AC

NOTE: These scenes are intended to be used for audition and class study; permission is not required to use the material for those purposes. However, if there is a paid performance of any of the scenes included in this book, please refer to the permissions acknowledgment pages to locate the source who can grant permission for public performance.

PASSING TIME

Your skin like dawn
mine like dusk.

One paints the beginning
of a certain end.

The other, the end of a
sure beginning.

Maya Angelou

FOR LYNNE ALVAREZ
AND IN MEMORY OF CHARLENE BLETSON

TABLE OF CONTENTS

SCENES FOR TWO WOMEN

SCENES FOR TWO MEN

SCENES FOR GROUPS

PREFACE

Multicultural Scenes and its companion book of monologues offers you a collection of material representative of the rich and varied cultures that make up our world. As with our previous collections, the selections are age-appropriate and depict obstacles that confront the young. Above all, we have carefully chosen works that will challenge and expand the depth of your experience both as an actor and as a human being.

We ask that you enter the lives of the characters you find here with wonderment and above all an open heart. Look for the similarities in the diversity of culture, for too often we dwell on the differences. Explore the patterns that tie us together, examine the threads that run through humankind, and revel in the brilliance of the colors in the tapestry of life. The invitation is, as the old saying goes, to walk in the shoes of others you encounter here. Indeed, this is the great invitation which every actor must accept: to crawl into the skin of another—to breathe life into the fictional creation, the dream issue of the dramatist—to transform self, and by so doing to illuminate the essence of what it means to be a human being.

If you accept the invitation fully with passion and commitment, if you read and study the complete texts from which the selections are taken, if you say "yes" to the creative curiosity burning within you, and if you continue to develop your instrument well, the journey upon which you have chosen to embark promises broad vistas, verdant valleys, and the highest peaks imaginable.

Craig Slaight, Jack Sharrar
San Francisco
October, 1994

INTRODUCTION

Multicultural Scenes for Young Actors is an artistic road map spanning time, continents, emotion, culture, gender, and history. The importance of this kind of expanse is that it will open up worlds that are simultaneously familiar and foreign. It will give young actors the opportunity to express and compare their life experiences: the nurturing of friendship, betrayal, the frustration of being trapped in the present by the past, the dreams of a life better than their parents, the sweetness and torture of crossing from child to adult, the loss of virginity, first love, faith in themselves, God and those around them, the fear of the world outside one's sphere of reference, justice, the powerful, the powerless, compassion for nature, and developing a sense of religion or ritual and on and on and on. The leaps within the material emotionally, culturally and trans-continently are striking in that they reflect with great accuracy and joy the world young actors live in and probably the classrooms in which they are participants.

Passion is a large part of being young. And passion is a large part of the scenes selected for this collection by some of the most gifted writers from around the world: Mary Gallagher, Lynne Alvarez, August Wilson, Charles Gordone, John M. Synge, Lorraine Hansberry, Horton Foote, Lanford Wilson, Mustapha Matura, Mikhail Roschin and David Henry Hwang to name but a few. As an example of what this study does, Renaldo Ferradas' *Birds Without Wings* expresses just how available that passion is when you are young, and the fear youth has of the monstrous results that passion can achieve.

> CARLOS: I carry the fire inside my skin. That fire that spread out inside this house to destroy everything.
> CLAUDIA: I'm afraid.
> CARLOS: I'm sorry. I didn't mean to scare you. They were here.
> CLAUDIA: Who are you talking about?
> CARLOS: My parents.
> CLAUDIA: Please don't turn yourself into Frankenstein?

Even youth such as the leader of the SHARKS or TYBALT, have felt ignored and "dis"-respected. They shout with graffiti, violence, music and, of course anger, "Look at me! I am a part of this world."

> CLAUDIA: Why did you mug me?
> CARLOS: You never looked at me.
> CLAUDIA: I never saw you.
> CARLOS: That's why I did it.

Passion runs deep when you are young and the body is often the tool used to express that passion.

> CARLOS: Do you want a little piece?
> CLAUDIA: I'd give my virginity to the man, only to the man who would love me.
> CARLOS: Why?
> CLAUDIA: The teacher with the big moustache... told us that the body is something sacred, that we have to be aware of whom we share it with. That it could harm us if we gave ourselves to the first man who asked for it.
> CARLOS: The son of a bitch convinced you.
> Claudia: I think he's right. Sex has a meaning when there is love. Without it, we'd stop being human.
> CARLOS (grabbing his genitals): What do I do with this?
> CLAUDIA: Do what you've been doing until now.
> (Carlos approaches without control. He is possessed by desire. He embraces Claudia and tries to kiss her. She pushes him away.) You're an animal, a donkey! That's what you are. Leave me alone.
> CARLOS: If you insult me I'll kill you.

It is often said that youth is wasted on the young. Perhaps it is, but not to the artist as a young man or young woman. They are being trained to look deeply and honestly within themselves, to express truthfully what they find there; their fears, longings, joys, and dreams, and then to rearrange them to fit a character, some-one else's personality, perspectives and situation. *Who am I? Where am I going? Whom do I expect to meet? What do I want from that person* and *To what extent am I willing to go to get it?*

Multicultural Scenes for Young Actors sets the stage for these questions to be asked, answered and enacted.

—*Joe Morton*

SCENES FOR ONE WOMAN AND ONE MAN

Birds Without Wings
By Renaldo Ferradas

Claudia, 16; Carlos, 18

Renaldo Ferradas' compelling play concerns two teenagers in a Cuban neighborhood in New York who find themselves in a mutual search for survival. Carlos, an orphan, is taken in by Claudia's family, who traffic in selling crack. The dysfunctional family, which relies on Claudia and Carlos to help in their criminal life, bring the two fearful youths together – at first as allies who shun the abuse from Claudia's parents – and later, as lovers. The struggle here is to survive not just in a troubled world but also the irresponsible and dangerous world of adult guardians and parents.

In the first scene, having met in a street encounter, Carlos has invited Claudia to see the burned-out remains of the apartment in which his family perished.

CLAUDIA: How much further do we have to go?

CARLOS: We've arrived. It's here.

CLAUDIA: There?

CARLOS: Yes, it's here. Come up. With three steps or four stepping stones, you will arrive at what is my holy place. Come in. Make yourself at home.

CLAUDIA: Do you live here?

CARLOS: As a child, I grew up here.

CLAUDIA: Even though I can't see it, I can still smell the smoke and feel the fire.

CARLOS: I carry the fire inside my skin. That fire that spread out inside this house to destroy everything.

CLAUDIA: I'm afraid.

CARLOS: I'm sorry. I didn't mean to scare you. They were here.

CLAUDIA: Who are you talking about?

CARLOS: My parents.

CLAUDIA: Please, don't turn yourself into Frankenstein.

CARLOS: Don't you remember anything from your childhood?

CLAUDIA: The only thing I remember was the day that mother went to the market and left me alone in the house, and I tried to fry some eggs and I burned my right hand. Look, there's still a scar from the burn.

CARLOS: Your skin was destroyed and your body was able to recreate the cells that were needed to grow new skin over the burned skin. My parents were never recreated. They went away once and for all. The last I remember of them is in this room. (*By this time, they are already inside the shell of what once was an apartment. Through the window at a distance, we can see burned-out or abandoned buildings.*) Mother and father were sleeping in a king-size bed. I was sleeping in the other room next to my older brother. (*He walks toward the hallway and points out the door frame.*) Here.

CLAUDIA: How lucky you are to have a brother. I'm alone!

CARLOS: I'm alone, too.

CLAUDIA: Where is your brother?

CARLOS: When smoke filled the room, the flames turned the heavy bricks into an oven. My brother quickly took me out of the bed where I was sleeping. He carried me in his arms with such tenderness that, still to this day, I carry it inside myself. Never again have I felt so much love. That's the last I remember of them. Later on, I lived in a vague silence of solitude marked by interviews of social workers, of unknown people, people who were unable to tell me if my name was Carlos or Charles. All of it was very strange.

CLAUDIA: Who do you live with?

CARLOS: With my grandmother.

CLAUDIA: Oh! Then you're not as lonely as you pretend to be.

CARLOS: I'm lonelier than what you might imagine.

CLAUDIA: Do you come here often?

CARLOS: This is the first time that I have come here in ten years. I thought I had forgotten how to get here. But you gave me the incentive to do this.

CLAUDIA: I?

CARLOS: Yes, you. When I saw you at the subway station, inside of me I felt a very strong desire. Suddenly, I found that I needed ties that would bring us together. I realized that probably you had an awful image of me. I wanted to wipe out those bad thoughts.

CLAUDIA: Why did you try to mug me?

CARLOS: You never looked at me.

CLAUDIA: I never saw you.

CARLOS: That's why I did it. I had to show you I was alive, that I was not a piece of stone or a floor one stands on, the one that keeps us from falling, and the one we rarely see. We walk without knowing the color or texture of what keeps us going.

CLAUDIA: I go to school to study. If you had watched me, you would have realized that I never look at anyone in particular.

CARLOS: You stare at the teacher with the big moustache. You're always looking at him.

CLAUDIA: I like him.

CARLOS: Why? Because he knows more than you and I?

CLAUDIA: He's our teacher.

CARLOS: (*Touching his genitals.*) In the field of masturbation, I know more than he does.

CLAUDIA: Stop being fresh with me.

CARLOS: Do you want a little piece?

CLAUDIA: I'd give my virginity to the man, only to the man who would love me.

CARLOS: Why?

CLAUDIA: That teacher with the big moustache did. (*She hesitates.*) He told us in one of his classes. He told us that the body is something sacred, that we have to be aware of whom we share it with. That it could harm us if we gave ourselves to the first man who asked for it.

CARLOS: The son of a bitch was able to convince you.

CLAUDIA: I think he's right. Sex has a meaning when there is love. Without it, we'd stop being human.

CARLOS: (*Grabbing his genitals.*) What do I do with this?

CLAUDIA: Do what you've been doing until now. (*Carlos approaches without control. He is possessed by desire. He embraces Claudia and tries to kiss her. She pushes him away.*) You're an animal, a donkey! That's what you are. Leave me alone. Don't fuck with my virginity, you son of a bitch.

CARLOS: If you insult me, I'll kill you.

CLAUDIA: Another death, Carlitos?

CARLOS: Yes, another. (*Claudia begins to run like a gazelle followed by a tiger. At full speed, she runs down to the ground floor. Carlos runs a few steps behind her. When they exit to the street, Claudia keeps on running. Carlos stops.*) Claudia! Claudia, Claudia, don't leave. Claudia, I was only kidding. It was a joke. (*Claudia stops in front of a street light. The noise of car motors and horns takes over the stage. Carlos takes advantage of the occasion to get closer. From a short distance he talks to Claudia.*) Forgive me, Claudia. I've brought you down to my parent's old apartment because I love you.

CLAUDIA: Love me? What you want to do is shake it, to masturbate it, son of a bitch, satyr!

CARLOS: Why don't you try to understand me? I'm alone, Claudia.

CLAUDIA: Get the love of your grandmother.

CARLOS: That old woman is not related to me. She gets paid for giving me shelter. For the last ten years she's been living off me. I'm her only subsistence. When I graduate next June, I'll be eighteen and I'll leave that apartment. That damn apartment! Claudia, listen, Claudia.

CLAUDIA: (*Carlos still a few steps away.*) I don't believe you.

CARLOS: You'll have to believe me. She's already searching for a way to find another victim to take my place when I leave. In that house there is nothing to eat, there's nothing there. As a child, I went hungry and I was cold. She's into gambling and that's how she spends all the money she gets. Do you understand why I have to sell drugs?

CLAUDIA: I sell them to help my parents.

CARLOS: I do it for my own help.

CLAUDIA: I'm not as lucky as you. I have no one to trust.

CARLOS: Whom do I have to trust?

CLAUDIA: Your brother, talk to him.

CARLOS: He's dead.

CLAUDIA: Another of your inventions.

CARLOS: I swear that I'm not lying to you. When my brother, Julio, realized that the fire was engulfing us inside the apartment, he placed a blanket around my body and in his arms he brought me down by the fire escape stairs. He left me in the hands of some people who had gathered to watch the fire. With love, he looked me in the eyes and with tenderness he kissed my forehead and said, "Don't worry, I'm going in to get our parents," and he never returned.

CLAUDIA: I don't understand why you have brought me here to this place so filled with unpleasant memories, with horrible things. I don't understand you.

CARLOS: If you could understand how much I like you, would you understand me?

CLAUDIA: Liking me? For sure, you are comparing me with a dummy in a window, one which you could use at will without any interest about what that dummy, if alive, would say.

CARLOS: Do you want me to punish myself because I wanted to give my body what I like? Claudia, I'm no masochist.

CLAUDIA: If we're to become friends, you must learn to control yourself. (*Carlos realizes that there is an opportunity to regain Claudia's friendship and to conquer her and he takes advantage of the situation, as they approach the grade school he attended, to change the conversation.*)

CARLOS: (*Pointing toward the distance.*) There, it's that school, I went to first and second grades. At that time, this neighborhood was populated by families, by workers like my father. We had many friends. Those were my best years. Father and mother were alive. I was going to school. My teachers were interested in me. They showed respect and love. At school there were monthly parties. We had balloon parties, funny hat parties, and sometimes famous people from the world of art. Musicians and singers came to entertain us. The teachers used to participate in the end of school year like it was today. One time mother made a clown costume for the principal of the school. He jumped and jumped like a monkey.

Life was so different from what it is today.

CLAUDIA: It must have been. Then, you didn't know how to masturbate.

CARLOS: I started doing it when I was four or five. When did you start?

CLAUDIA: I don't do those things.

CARLOS: Let me see your right hand.

CLAUDIA: I'm left-handed.

CARLOS: You're a devil.

CLAUDIA: Damn you!

CARLOS: Kiss me.

CLAUDIA: I will only kiss the man who offers me eternal fidelity.

CARLOS: Do you want to come with me?

CLAUDIA: Where do you want to take me?

CARLOS: To Hunt's Point.

CLAUDIA: What is there?

CARLOS: A beautiful beach where my parents used to take me when I was a child. Today, I feel melancholic, I wish to share with you my innermost secrets. Come with me. (*The youngsters hold hands and walk. During their walk, they encounter burnt-out and rundown buildings and vacant lots. By the entrance of some buildings, cardboard women, human size, appear. They are wearing overcoats. When Claudia and Carlos approach, these women open their coats and appear totally naked.*)

CLAUDIA: Your parents brought you here?

CARLOS: It wasn't like this then.

CLAUDIA: My parents are right when they say that everything has changed.

CARLOS: (*Pointing to the beach.*) There was never shit floating in the sea.

CLAUDIA: Don't be gross.

CARLOS: I don't disrespect you, Claudia. Look and tell me what you see. What do you see floating out there?

CLAUDIA: The sun is setting, but I swear that it's shit on the beach. Without any doubt, it is shit.

CARLOS: If you say so, I can't argue with you.

CLAUDIA: It's an ugly word.

CARLOS: It seems ugly to you because it reminds you of the beast inside you.

CLAUDIA: I think you're right.

CARLOS: Then why did you call me an animal a while ago? Why did you call me a donkey?

CLAUDIA: Because you don't know how to control your instincts.

CARLOS: Then for my next reincarnation, I'll ask the universe to send me back as a horse or a panther. They fuck whenever they feel like it.

CLAUDIA: You're so gross!

CARLOS: Hypocrite.

CLAUDIA: (*Looking at her watch.*) I have to go. It's later than I thought.

CARLOS: What are you going to do for Easter Week?

CLAUDIA: Pray for your soul.

CARLOS: Liar!

CLAUDIA: I have the soul of a nun.

CARLOS: If that's true, then stop masturbating.

CLAUDIA: How did you know?

CARLOS: (*Grabbing her left hand.*) Mother of God! You're growing a callous! (*Carlos and Claudia burst out laughing as they embrace. Blackout.*)

◆ ◆ ◆ ◆

Claudia, 16; Carlos, 18

In this scene, Claudia and Carlos consider a life together apart from the struggle and ruin of their present existence – they share the dream of the quality life they both desire.

Claudia and Carlos look at the Hudson River and plan what they want to do with their lives. At a distance we hear the final notes of a soprano singing "O Patria Mia," from the opera Aida, *then the applause.*

CLAUDIA: I like salsa better.

CARLOS: I do too, but this crowd doesn't seem to be silly or stupid at all. Do you know who is sitting there next to that very attractive woman?

CLAUDIA: Who?

CARLOS: Your favorite teacher, the one with the big moustache. Do you see him? He's right there. (*He points with his finger.*) He's leaving.

CLAUDIA: (*Nodding.*) Then it must be a very important concert. If I had seen him before, I would have liked to say hello. By the way, Carlos, in yesterday's class he told the class that it was important to receive letters from the people we love. That way we can measure their spiritual and intellectual capacity. So, Carlos, what are you waiting for to write me a letter?

CARLOS: Why should I do that, when we sleep together?

CLAUDIA: Carlos, in two weeks you'll graduate from high school. I want to learn from you.

CARLOS: You still haven't learned to write a letter?

CLAUDIA: I want to learn from you. I want you to teach me everything you know.

CARLOS: Don't think that I know that much more than you.

CLAUDIA: The teacher with the big moustache, as you call him, is the only one who corrects the homework. Most of the time, I don't know if I answer the questions right or wrong.

CARLOS: You ought to spend more time at the library, like me. That's where I learned words like "laissez-faire."

CLAUDIA: What does it mean?

CARLOS: It means the government has no control or the right to interfere in any kind of business. Do you hear?

CLAUDIA: I feel guilty.

CARLOS: The police do it! Everyone we know does it. Why shouldn't we do it?

CLAUDIA: I never used it until you taught me.

CARLOS: Are you trying to pull the wool over my eyes?

CLAUDIA: I swear!

CARLOS: We have to set up our own nest far from grandmother

spider. She's the one who's making the money.

CLAUDIA: But we are not learning because we're high all the time.

CARLOS: I still go to the library.

CLAUDIA: To sell.

CARLOS: And you go to the girls' lockers.

CLAUDIA: To sell for grandmother spider.

CARLOS: The first thing we have to do is get away. To get away from it all. Do you accept my proposition?

CLAUDIA: Only if we celebrate our wedding in the garden of the Spanish cloister.

CARLOS: Why there and not in another place?

CLAUDIA: That place means a lot to me, Carlos. As a little girl, from my window in my bedroom there (*She points to the distance.*) I used to look toward this building and I felt like Prince Valiant's girlfriend waiting for him to honor me by coming down from his Middle Ages palace to ask for my hand.

CARLOS: Are you old enough to get married?

CLAUDIA: I'm only sixteen, but we don't have to tell them the truth. Why do you want to get married?

CARLOS: Because I'm planning to join the army and I want you to come with me to know the world. Somehow traveling has attracted me. Do you see that bird flying there in the distance? I envy it more than I envy any other animal. With its wings, it can transport itself to any place. When we get married, if you wish, you could join the army, too. Between the two of us, we could earn a good salary and we could save enough to buy ourselves a small plane.

CLAUDIA: Carlos, I can't leave my parents abandoned in jail.

CARLOS: Do you love them that much?

CLAUDIA: Why should it surprise you? I've always told you that my parents were the best parents in the world.

CARLOS: How old were you when you started to sell crack?

CLAUDIA: Ten years old.

CARLOS: Who initiated you into this?

CLAUDIA: My parents never used any kind of drugs. I told you. They never started me in any wrong thing. You know very well that they used to sell it because they were trying to get away from this evil neighborhood. Everyone does it in this area.

CARLOS: Everyone?

CLAUDIA: Everyone we know. When we moved into that building there, Mother used to clean office buildings, Father used to work as a waiter. Slowly, they discover that their neighbors were earning three times as much as they did. Those neighbors convinced my parents to leave their jobs and dedicate themselves to an easy life. The police used to enter and exit from these people's house without any arrest. The first time that Mother witnessed that she was terrified until our neighbor told her that it was a routine. The police came and went to collect their tax. That's why I'm surprised that they are in jail. It must have been a report. If I ever find out who did that thing, I swear to you that I'll tear them apart with my bare hands.

CARLOS: Where is all the money that they earned?

CLAUDIA: I forgot to tell you. Mother confessed that it was in a safe deposit box at the bank. The police confiscated it.

CARLOS: Damn it!

CLAUDIA: Why in the world am I so goddamned lucky as to have a family so different from any other?

CARLOS: My family was great.

CLAUDIA: That's why you are so wonderful.

CARLOS: Do you really think so?

CLAUDIA: I really do, Carlos.

CARLOS: I don't know how in the world I have given you that impression. My life has been filled with mosaics, with fragments of remembrances, with impossibilities of achievements, I feel like a bird without wings. I want to fly and I can't. Everything is denied to me.

CLAUDIA: Everything is possible if we only try.

CARLOS: Maybe you're right. Maybe we still have a chance.

CLAUDIA: Yes, we can still make something out of our lives. I hardly can write well, Carlos. You know, at times I think that we are different. You and I are not white with blue eyes and light skin. I think that to the teachers of another culture, we are worthless.

CARLOS: In the army, everything will be different. I used to want to be a baseball player, but I was too short for that. When I went to the medical center to visit their endocrinologist clinic, the doctor told me that my bones had already grown enough. He assured me that I had no problem of dwarfism and that my pituitary gland was working all right. Does it bother you that I'm shorter than you?

CLAUDIA: You're my Adam.

CARLOS: You're my Eve.

CARLOS/CLAUDIA: What should we do with paradise?

CARLOS: Let's destroy everything.

CLAUDIA: Why?

CARLOS: Because we are too far from paradise, Claudia. Let's go.

CLAUDIA: I don't want to leave this sunset. Look at it, isn't it marvelous? (*The sun is setting and the light changes the illumination of the afternoon.*)

CARLOS: That is an illusion of life, Claudia. Is the sun what we believe to be the sun, and the one in which we place our hopes for the future? For the rich it's a promise of luxury and greediness. For the poor like you and me, it is a promise of deprivations. For the fools who believe in heaven and hell, it is a promise of a better life. What has man done? We have traveled to the moon. We have built telescopes that can see nebulae that ceased to exist long ago. Meanwhile, here on earth we can't even eat a chicken. Everything is poisoned, cattle and fish, fruits and vegetables. And the last thing which we have left, the warmth of a body next to ours, it's also a putrefying thought. With all this thing about AIDS, I waited until I found a woman like you so I could give myself to life. Do you understand? I chose you because I knew you were not a prostitute. I never saw you whoring with anybody in school. If your parents get out, would you leave me for them?

CLAUDIA: I love them, but I wouldn't leave you.

CARLOS: (*Embracing Claudia.*) Your parents were strange trunks. By their own effort they never got anywhere. Their branches only gave a single flower. You.

CLAUDIA: Father told me recently that he and Mama grew up together in the mountains. Since then, I ask myself, are they brother and sister? Are they my real parents?

CARLOS: Let's destroy the flowers and the trees, let's destroy the stinking air smelling of gasoline. Let's destroy earth. Let's destroy the fish and the sea. Let's destroy the heavens and the faraway galaxies. Let's destroy the sun and moon. How about a suicide pact?

CLAUDIA: You kill yourself. I don't want to die.

CARLOS: Don't you realize that it is not worth it to keep on living if we don't even know where we came from or where we're going. Don't you realize how sad it is to know so little about the ones who brought us into the world?

CLAUDIA: You're crazy. A while ago you asked me to marry you. Later we planned to travel to visit faraway worlds and suddenly you want to destroy everything. What the fuck is happening to you?

CARLOS: Claudia, tell me the truth, does it bother you that I'm shorter than you?

CLAUDIA: Until now, I had not realized it.

CARLOS: If you never wear high heels, and I wear them, and if you tie your hair up close to your scalp, you'll only be a little taller than me. (*They kiss. Blackout.*)

Bitter Cane
By Genny Lim

Wing Chung Kuo, 16; Li-Tai, mid-30s

Genny Lim's *Bitter Cane* is set in Hawaii in the mid-1800s and concerns the coming of age of sixteen-year-old Wing Chung Kuo, a Chinese immigrant who's come to the islands to work on a sugar cane plantation. Like so many before him, Wing believes that the freedom and potential riches to be gained by working in this new land will be a welcome elevation, far superior to the meager existence in his homeland village in China.

Wing discovers, however, that the exploitation of the Chinese immigrants leads to indulgent and destructive behavior, as evidenced by the reckless activities of the older workers who spend all of their free time gambling, smoking opium and paying for sexual favors from prostitutes. The play follows Wing's journey into manhood in a most theatrical way, including scenes with the ghost of Wing's father, who too was a sugar cane cutter and died shaming his family.

In this first scene, Wing is led to the room of Li-Tai, a local prostitute, hoping for his first adult experience with a woman. Lau Hing Juo, the ghost of Wing's father, shadows Wing through the scene – he too was a partner of Li-Tai in life.

◆ ◆ ◆ ◆

LI-TAI: (*Calling from inside.*) Who is it?

WING: (*Clearing his throat.*) My name is Wing Chun…Kuo.
    (*The light inside the cabin comes up as Li-Tai slowly opens the door. She motions him to enter. He stands there awkwardly.*)

LI-TAI: (*Stares at him with immediate recognition.*) You?

WING: (*Captivated.*) I hope it's not too late.

LI-TAI: (*Glancing around nervously.*) I thought I heard voices.
    (*Returning curiously to Wing.*) You new?

WING: Yes. Three weeks.

LI-TAI: Hoi-ping?

WING: (*Surprised.*) Yes. How did you know?

LI-TAI: (*Matter-of-factly.*) By the way you talk.

WING: (*Impressed.*) You're clever.

LI-TAI: (*Examining him.*) You're good-looking. You look mixed.

WING: I'm Chinese, same as you. I was the best farmer back home.

LI-TAI: I believe it. (*Looks at his hands.*) Are you good with your hands?

WING: (*Surprised.*) Yes. I can carve things.

LI-TAI: (*Impressed.*) Ah, an artist! (*Sounding his name.*) Wing Chun. My name is Li-Tai.

WING: Li-Tai. That's pretty. (*Pauses.*) Where you from?

LI-TAI: (*Abruptly.*) Look. I know you're not here to gossip. You have two dollars? (*He fumbles in his pocket and without looking hands her several bills. She smirks at his naïveté and quickly tucks it in her kimono pocket.*) Sit down. (*He sits.*) Want something to drink?

WING: Some tea would be nice, thank you.

LI-TAI: (*Amused laugh.*) Tea? How old are you?

WING: Twenty.

LI-TAI: (*Frowning.*) You're lying.

WING: (*Embarrassed.*) Sixteen.

LI-TAI: This is your first time? (*He nods with embarrassment. She takes a whiskey bottle, uncorks it, pours a glass, and hands it to him.*) Drink it. It'll give you confidence. (*He takes a big swallow and chokes. She laughs at him.*) Slow down. What's your hurry? (*Smiling.*) Talk to me.

WING: (*Still embarrassed.*) About what?

LI-TAI: About you.

WING: (*Blushing.*) There's not much to tell.

LI-TAI: Why not?

WING: (*Takes a gulp, then blurts . . .*) My name is Wing and I like to eat duck gizzards. (*She bursts out laughing, then he laughs, too.*) On the first day of school, I remember the teacher asked us to introduce ourselves.

LI-TAI: And that was what you said.

WING: I couldn't think of anything else!

LI-TAI: (*Mockingly.*) You still can't.

WING: (*Frustrated.*) I don't know why I'm so tongue-tied. (*Finishes his glass.*)

LI-TAI: Talking is not important. (*Refills his glass.*) There are other ways to communicate. (*Pours herself one, clicks his glass, then slumps on the bed with her glass in a provocative manner.*) Your parents have a bride picked out for you yet?

WING: No. (*Pauses.*) My parents are dead.

LI-TAI: I'm sorry.

WING: My father died here. At Kahuku.

LI-TAI: Oh? (*Surprised.*) What was his name?

WING: Lau Hing. Kuo Lau Hing. (*She freezes at the recognition of his name.*) He was one of those Sandalwood boys who never made it back.

LI-TAI: (*Trembling.*) How old were you when he left?

WING: I was just a baby.

(*Struck by the resemblance, she cups his face with her hands.*)

LI-TAI: Let me look at you!

WING: (*Embarrassed.*) What's the matter? Why are you looking at me like that?

LI-TAI: (*Marveling.*) You remind me of someone.

WING: I'm as good as any man on Kahuku.

LI-TAI: (*Disdainfully.*) The average man here is a pig. You don't want to be like them, do you?

WING: One flop in the family is enough. It's no secret. Lau Hing was a bum.

LI-TAI: How can a son talk about his own father in that way?

WING: And how can a father treat his family that way? Why should I pretend he was somebody he wasn't? (*Somberly.*) He was nobody to me. Nothing.

LI-TAI: (*Stung with guilt.*) Your mother? She loved him?

WING: (*Disgustedly.*) She died. He lied to her. He lied to her every month for two years! When he got tired of lying, he stopped writing altogether. She didn't hear from him again. Then one day, she gets this letter saying he's dead. (*Bitterly.*) You want to know what killed him? (*Pauses.*) Opium. The money he should have sent home, he squandered on himself! (*Pauses.*) They shipped his trunk back. She thought it was his bones. When she opened it, she fainted. The box was empty except for his hat and a few personal belongings. His body was never recovered they said, because he had drowned in the ocean. (*With cruel irony.*) That's why I'm here. To redeem a dead man.

LI-TAI: You think you'll succeed?

WING: I'm not sending my ghost in an empty box home. Life is too short! (*Listening to the sound of rain.*) It's raining again.

LI-TAI: It's always raining. There's no escape. (*With a sense of foreboding.*) You do what you can do to forget. And survive. (*Picks up a fan and begins moodily fanning herself.*) I can't decide what's more boring. Living out here in the middle of nowhere or raising chickens in a puny plot back home.

WING: Why did you come here?

LI-TAI: A lady in the village told me that Hawai'i was paradise. She said there was hardly anything to do there but suck on big, fat, juicy sugarcane – sweeter than honey. I was crazy for cane and waited for the day to come here. When my mother died, my father remarried. My new mother didn't like a girl with bound feet who talked back. So I told her to send me to Hawai'i. She sold me to a rich old merchant on the Big Island. I cried and begged to go back home. But I was his number four concubine. His favorite. Four is a bad luck number. So when the old man suffered a stroke in my bedroom, they, of course, blamed it on me. Number one wife, who was always jealous of me, picked up my red slippers and threw them at my face. Then she beat me with a bamboo rod and called me a good-for-nothing slave girl! (*Laughs bitterly.*) They lit firecrackers when Fook Ming took me. To rid my evil spirit. Some paradise. (*Moved by Wing's look of compassion.*) Tell me, what do they say about me?

WING: (*Blushing.*) Who?

LI-TAI: The men. What do the men say about Li-Tai?

(*Lau Hing crosses from the wing toward Li-Tai.*)

WING: Nothing. (*Admiringly.*) Just that you're beautiful.

[LAU: (*Passionately.*) You're beautiful! (*Li-Tai turns and sees Lau.*)]

LI-TAI: Who sent you here?

WING: No one, I swear!

LI-TAI: (*Frightened by Lau's apparition.*) Why do you come? (*Cautiously.*) What do you want from me?

WING: (*Apologetic and earnest.*) I came to you because I need a woman.

[LAU: (*Echoing simultaneously.*) I came to you because I need a woman.]

LI-TAI: (*Scornfully.*) How much is your pleasure worth? Two dollars? All the money you have?

WING: (*Ardently.*) Everything!

[LAU: Everything!]

LI-TAI: (*With a nervous laugh.*) So you need a woman. But not just any woman? (*Crosses to a table and lights a candle in a glass holder.*) You want one with experience? One who can guide you into manhood? (*Puts out the kerosene lamp, picks up the candle, and turns to him.*) Someone who can open your eyes and wipe the clouds from them. (*Crosses to him.*) Because you're not a little boy anymore. (*Continues her cross to the bed.*) And Mama can't help you. (*Places candle on bedside table, then lies down.*) But I can. (*Coyly.*) Come here. (*He takes a nervous breath and crosses to her. He halts in front of her. Lau turns and watches them.*) Are you afraid of me? (*She reaches for him and pulls him down to his knees. She puts his hand to her face and he slowly strokes her cheek as if discovering a woman's skin for the first time. He continues touching and stroking her face, neck, arms, and shoulders, gently and innocently.*) You're pure as the lily's hidden leaf. (*Gazing intently at him.*) I see little torches flickering in your eyes!

WING: (*With nervous passion.*) They burn for you.

LI-TAI: You should stay away from fire.

WING: Why? We sacrifice to the gods with fire.

LI-TAI: Forget the gods. There's only you and I here. And the huge ocean, which surrounds us. (*She pulls him to her. She takes his hands and examines them as if remembering something from the past. She gently presses them to her cheeks. Then she pulls him alongside her on the bed. He removes her*

embroidered slippers, gently, then caresses her feet. Lau
approaches the pair, mesmerized.)

WING: Does that feel good? (*She moans softly.*) They're so tiny.

LI-TAI: (*Sighs.*) Oh your hands . . . they feel like water!

[LAU: (*Echoing*) . . . they feel like water!]

LI-TAI: (*Matter-of-factly.*) I'm made for pleasure. Not marriage.
Family, cooking, raising babies. I wouldn't be good for that. (*A
sad laugh.*) I'm only good for one thing. (*Provocatively.*) And
you, what are you good for?

◆ ◆ ◆ ◆

Wing Chung Kuo, 16; Li-Tai, mid-30s

In the next scene, the morning following, Wing awakes late, startled he spent the
night with Li-Tai.

WING: (*Looks around, disoriented, then horrified.*) Oh my god, it's
morning! How could I fall asleep! (*Gets up and starts
frantically putting on his clothes.*) I gotta get back.

LI-TAI: (*Calmly.*) Wait. I'll fix breakfast. You can't work on an empty
stomach.

WING: Next time.

LI-TAI: (*Resolutely.*) Maybe there won't be a next time.

WING: (*Confused.*) I don't understand.

LI-TAI: (*A bit forcefully.*) Stay here.

WING: I can't. (*Reassuringly.*) Look, I'll be back.

LI-TAI: (*Skeptically.*) When?

WING: Next Saturday?

LI-TAI: (*Demanding.*) Tomorrow!

WING: (*Embarrassed.*) I-I . . . can't afford . . .

LI-TAI: (*Offended.*) I won't take your money. I don't want it. Just
don't treat me like some whore.

WING: (*Taking her by the shoulder.*) What's gotten into you?

LI-TAI: (*Pulling away.*) You tell me. (*Sarcastically.*) You're a man. Oh
what's the use! The sun flattens down on you like an iron and

all you can do is lie there and whimper. (*A sigh of disgust.*)
Some paradise.

WING: You give in to bitterness.

LI-TAI: They said, "You will never want to leave!" (*With bitter
irony.*) I never asked to come. (*Reminiscing.*) I was only twenty
when I came to Kahuku . . . (*Turning away from him.*) . . . and
the easy life. I've been here too long! (*Gesturing at the
landscape.*) Like those mountains that never move. (*Thinking
aloud.*) What do you think happens to us when we die?

WING: (*Decisively.*) We go on living in the afterlife.

LI-TAI: No we don't. We wither and die.

WING: Don't you believe in immortality?

LI-TAI: (*Firmly.*) No.

WING: Everything lives in the soul.

LI-TAI: Everything dies in the heart.

WING: That's not Chinese!

LI-TAI: Maybe I'm not Chinese.

WING: Don't you believe in fate?

LI-TAI: No.

WING: Why not?

LI-TAI: Because fate is destiny. I don't believe in destiny. It's our
own hand that pulls us down, not some god's. We answer to
ourselves.

WING: I don't know about that . . . (*Romantically*) I was lying in the
dark, unable to sleep, so I listened to sounds. The soft feet of
rain, the rustling of boughs and leaves, ten thousand voices of
crickets . . . I heard the grass talk to the wind. I heard the
cicada's song.

LI-TAI: (*Amused.*) What did it sing?

WING: It sang good evening to the stars.

LI-TAI: And what did the stars answer?

WING: The stars answered that they were lonely.

LI-TAI: Why were they lonely?

WING: Because they shined alone in the sky.

LI-TAI: (*Laughing.*) Did they sing in Chinese?

WING: In a language beyond words. Did you ever try, when you were a kid, to pick out one star in the sky, then try to find that same star the next night? You can't. But you keep looking anyhow. When I first looked at you, I had this feeling fate brought us together. (*Looks at her meaningfully.*) Things happen for a reason.

LI-TAI: I don't believe that. Things just happen. We make them happen. We stumble into traps. We live, we die.

WING: (*Intrigued.*) You're not like the women back home.

LI-TAI: They all think like one person. The young girls talk like old women and the old women are ignorant and superstitious. In China you're born old before you can walk. As a woman you're allowed to do only one thing. Please men. I've spent my whole life doing that! (*Matter-of-factly.*) You see this body? It's not mine. It belongs to Kahuku Plantation. My skin even smells like burnt cane!

WING: And what about your heart?

LI-TAI: I cut it out. Long ago.

WING: Then what was it I felt last night? (*With certainty.*) I've known you before.

LI-TAI: Last night I was drunk! So were you. (*Begins primping before the mirror.*) What happened to all the years? I look in the mirror and count each new gray hair. (*Sadly.*) Time has no respect for a woman.

WING: (*Looking at her reflection from behind.*) You have a beautiful face, a true face. With features that sing. (*Tenderly.*) Your brows describe the mists of Kweilin.

LI-TAI: (*Laughs.*) What do my wrinkles reveal?

WING: The soft rays of the moon.

LI-TAI: A waning moon?

WING: No. A full one. (*Dramatically.*) I was reborn last night.

LI-TAI: (*Laughing.*) Don't make me laugh.

WING: I mean it. (*Puts his arms shyly around her.*)

LI-TAI: Don't be foolish. (*Scoffing.*) I'm old enough to be your mother!

WING: The soul has no age.

LI-TAI: (*Sighs.*) You remind me of a man I loved fifteen years ago.

WING: Who was that?

LI-TAI: (*Elusively.*) A man who was a cicada. (*Thoughtfully.*) Did you know the cicada dies after he mates?

WING: (*Optimistically.*) Yes, but he is resurrected from the grave he leaves behind.

(*Wing kisses her, then exits.*)

Buba
By Hillel Mitelpunkt; Translated by Michael Taub

Rachel, 17, Elie, 30

A search for happiness, *Buba* dramatizes the story of the title character, a middle-aged Israeli who is in conflict with his brother and himself. In the course of the play Buba meets and falls in love with Rachel, a young wanderer.

Here, Rachel returns in the evening to Buba's shack, startled to find Elie waiting in the dark.

RACHEL: Didn't think anybody was here.

ELIE: I stand like this sometimes. Because of thieves.

RACHEL: Buba said I could come. Anytime I want. I can come.

ELIE: Buba left.

RACHEL: Yes?

ELIE: He'll be gone for a while. Maybe a week. (*Silence.*)

RACHEL: I'll wait for him here.

ELIE: No.

RACHEL: He said I could, anytime. If I want, I can come.

ELIE: He didn't tell me anything about it.

RACHEL: He told me this morning when we were walking to the main road. (*Elie comes closer, looks her over good. Takes her shopping bag, opens the door, and throws it out.*) You're crazy.

ELIE: Get out.

RACHEL: I don't want to.

ELIE: Get out of here.

RACHEL: This is Buba's place. (*Silence. He grabs her, drags her to the door. She fights back.*)

ELIE: Get out!

RACHEL: No. (*She bites his hand. He screams. He throws her out.*)

ELIE: Bitch . . . lousy bitch. (*They each push from their own side of the door.*)

RACHEL: Let me in.

ELIE: Shut up!

RACHEL: No I won't! I'll tell them you're here. You think I don't know who you are? If you don't let me in, I'll go and tell them.

ELIE: Shut your mouth!

RACHEL: They'll kill you! (*Silence, waits a minute, opens the door. She sits by the door, shoulder bag and tape player between her knees. Elie leaves the door open, she comes in.*) You almost ruined my clothes.

ELIE: One more word from you and I'll kill you. I'll bury you in the yard. Nobody will find out. Not even Buba.

RACHEL: I'll tell them about you. I'll tell them you're here.

ELIE: No you won't, because if you do, you're dead.

RACHEL: I will.

ELIE: Sit there. (*Rachel takes off her shirt, revealing a shiny dancer's top. She looks in the mirror.*)

RACHEL: You like it? I bought it for tomorrow's competition. It really shines in the light. I got it in a special store in Tel Aviv.

ELIE: Buba gave you money?

RACHEL: Even if he wanted to I wouldn't take it. Nobody paid for me in my whole life. I saved some money. I worked in a garment factory where they make slips.

ELIE: Slips . . .

RACHEL: That's right, slips. For old women. (*Silence.*) Where did he go?

ELIE: He has things to do.

RACHEL: I'm sure he went to see a friend. He said he has lots of friends.

ELIE: Sometimes he lies.

RACHEL: I thought so. He's nice to me, so what do I care?

ELIE: He once had a wife. And a kid.

RACHEL: I don't ask questions. (*Elie smiles.*) I'm not sure you're not making this up . . .

ELIE: When they got divorced, her lawyer said . . . something was wrong with his head. They didn't let him see his child. They gave him a soda stand when the main road was busy. A whole week he couldn't find the syrup, so one day he got mad, took the whole thing apart and built this shack.

RACHEL: Retarded people can't fix motorcycles.

ELIE: Yeah, did you see it? He only thinks he's fixing it. Sometimes I see his wife. She's lucky she found another husband.

RACHEL: I could tell he once lived with a woman. I can tell, you know.

ELIE: How?

RACHEL: Signs. I know. You can see on the body.

ELIE: What can you tell about me? (*Silence.*)

RACHEL: I knew right away something was wrong with him by his fingers. Somebody told me if the nails were square, something's wrong with the head. He said he worked in a garage. (*Silence.*) Is it true what he said, your name was in the papers?

ELIE: Come here.

RACHEL: What?

ELIE: Come here.

RACHEL: I don't want to. (*Silence.*) What?

ELIE: This is not a hotel, you know. I could tell you to go and I could tell you to stay.

RACHEL: So what if you can? Buba said I can stay.

ELIE: I'm not Buba. (*Goes to the table, opens the shopping bag, pulls out a jump-suit with shiny reflectors on it. She wants to take it away from him. He pulls her and the suit towards him. She falls on him and kisses him. Elie breaks away from her.*) Don't like it when they stick their tongues in my mouth. (*Gets a towel, throws it at her.*) Go, wash up first.

RACHEL: I'm clean. (*Goes to the sink, checks the water.*) Can't do it like this. The water's cold.

ELIE: Warm it up on the hotplate.

RACHEL: You wash with water from a pot. I didn't ask if you were dirty, did I? (*Slips into bed with him and covers herself up.*)

ELIE: (*Picks up the blanket and looks at her.*) A skeleton. What can you do?

RACHEL: Put on some music. It's quiet here, I think it's the end of the world. (*Elie turns on the tape player – disco music.*)

¿De Dónde?
By Mary Gallagher

Felicia, 18-20; Victor, 16-18

Mary Gallagher's compelling drama depicts the lives of Hispanics in the Rio Grande Valley of Texas and is concerned with the rights of refugees and their encounters with the INS (Immigration and Naturalization Service). The title refers to the shortened Spanish phrase for the question "Where are you from?" This is the first phrase heard by Hispanics suspected of being aliens.

In the scene below, Felicia, a Mexican-American valley native, befriends Victor, a Guatemalan refugee, whose family this evening has taken shelter (safe from the authorities) at Felicia's home.

FELICIA: Is your family resting?

VICTOR: Sleeping. You gave us so much food . . . after four days of walking . . . my sister fell asleep with her spoon like this! (*Thumb in mouth, laughs; sees Felicia doesn't.*) It's all right, I'll get them up when you want us to go.
(*Pause. Then Felicia sits on the floor, gestures for him to sit with her.*)

FELICIA: You're not sleepy?

VICTOR: I'm still seeing the river and the fields . . . and then the rows of houses . . . We couldn't believe it! Some of the houses here are so small and ugly, it almost looks like home.

FELICIA: Well, this neighborhood is hardly even Texas. Everybody's Mexican. The poor ones buy a little plot and slap a house together out of scrap, whatever they can find –

VICTOR: But your house is so beautiful, we almost passed it by – especially when we saw your new car.

FELICIA: That car's three years old.

VICTOR: All the cars in our village are falling apart. The gas tank in my uncle's car is just a bucket on the front seat – you don't light a cigarette, or – (*Explosion sound.*) . . . So when my father saw your car, he said, "These people will turn us in."

FELICIA: Why?

VICTOR: Because if you didn't, the security forces might come around later and take away your car.

FELICIA: . . . That's not the way it happens here.

VICTOR: That's what *I* said! And then my mother – she's very religious – she saw the little shrine to Our Lady in your garden, and she said it was a sign.

FELICIA: . . . I forgot it was even there . . . You want more cookies?

VICTOR: Yes, of course!

(Felicia goes offstage.)

VICTOR: I feel like I'm dreaming! We talked about this for so long . . . but my parents were scared. Not me – I was glad when the army burned our house down – finally we *had* to come!

(Victor laughs, amazed, as Felicia reenters with four bags of cookies.)

FELICIA: *(Enjoying his surprise.)* Why *did* they burn your house?

(She piles cookie bags in his arms, opens a bag and takes out cookies. As he answers her question, gradually she slows and stops.)

VICTOR: My father pissed them off. They were making all the men and boys in our village join the Civil Patrol . . . where we watch for the guerilla . . . and we have to give the army names of people who support them – even if we don't *know* anybody who supports them. And if the guerilla attack, we have to fight them – except we can't have guns!

FELICIA: Why not?

VICTOR: The army won't allow it, they think we'll shoot at *them*.

FELICIA: But then . . . how are you supposed to fight?

VICTOR: That's what my father said! And the army told him, "It's okay, just fight them with sticks and rocks." My father said, "Go fuck yourself!," so they burned our house. Oh – excuse my language, there.

FELICIA: Good for your father anyway.

VICTOR: We were surprised they didn't shoot us. But we had to go. It wasn't the house so much – we could have built another one, from scrap, like you were saying – but anytime, the army might have come back through and shot us, you know, if they'd remembered . . . so . . . the United States! I think everything is here! Like your shoes!

FELICIA: My shoes?

VICTOR: What do you call them?

FELICIA: Reeboks.

VICTOR: So beautiful! In Guatemala, they pay you so little, and the prices are so high, you could work your whole life, till you die crippled from the work, and you could never own a pair of shoes like that! And neither will your children. It'll be the same for them, never any better. But here in the United States, workers can have these shoes! And this – what is this machine?

FELICIA: (*Groping to explain.*) . . . It's for showing movies on the TV screen. So you can buy a movie and play it anytime you want –

VICTOR: We could play one *now?*

FELICIA: (*Hesitates.*) Well . . . they're all in English –

VICTOR: I love hearing English! Soon I'll understand it too! I'll go wake my family up – they have to see this!

FELICIA: No, wait . . .

VICTOR: (*Stops dead.*) You want us to go.

FELICIA: . . . No . . . but let them sleep, we'll wake them when my father gets home.

(*She takes his hand, they exit.*)

Eddie opunẉ Edmundo
By Lynne Alvarez

Alicia, 16; Eddie, 18

Lynne Alvarez's *Eddie opunẉ Edmundo* concerns the journey of a young Hispanic American who travels to Nautla, Mexico, in search of his family's past and his own future after the death of his mother. Confronted with deep conflicts between the culture in which he was raised (as a Hispanic in New York City) and the culture he faces in Mexico, Eddie seeks his true identity and a place in the world. Along the way he is touched and moved by his Aunt Chelo and her fiancé of many years, Nyin, and stirred with love for a local girl.

In the first scene, Eddie meets Alicia in the cafe that his Aunt Chelo owns.

ALICIA: Who are you?

EDDIE: Eddie.

ALICIA: Unhmmm. (*Pause.*) You from New York?

EDDIE: Yeah.

ALICIA: We have a saying – "Crazy as a goat in New York City." Is it like that?

EDDIE: What?

ALICIA: Crazy. Cars all over the place. Noise.

EDDIE: That's a pretty good description.

ALICIA: I'd hate it there.

EDDIE: I couldn't imagine you there.

ALICIA: Why not?

EDDIE: Give me fifty years and I'll tell you.

ALICIA: You think I'm ignorant?

EDDIE: No. No. It's just. Forget it.

ALICIA: Well. You don't belong here either.

EDDIE: Fine.

ALICIA: My name's Alicia. How old are you? I'm sixteen.

EDDIE: Old enough.

ALICIA: I have a boyfriend. My parents don't want me to marry him.

I don't know why not. My mother married at fourteen. (*Waits for a response. There is none.*) That's why I'm here. He'll come and get me though. Soon.

EDDIE: Good. I wish you luck.

ALICIA: Doña Chelo told you not to talk to me, didn't she?

EDDIE: Sort of.

ALICIA: And you're afraid of me.

EDDIE: Give me a break.

ALICIA: You'd make an excellent priest, you know. So much self-control. And so handsome . . . I always wondered why so many priests are handsome. What a waste. And they're embarrassed by everything. Nuns are never embarrassed. (*She looks at him.*) It's fun torturing you like this. Making you talk.

EDDIE: I'm not talking.

ALICIA: I heard your mother died. I'm sorry. I was trying to cheer you up. I'll leave you alone. Your name is Eduardo?

EDDIE: Edmundo. Eddie.

ALICIA: Oooooooooooo.

EDDIE: What?

ALICIA: You have a namesake in the village.

EDDIE: Yeah, who?

ALICIA: I'll give you a hint. Neither of you talks. But at least *he* sings.

◆ ◆ ◆ ◆

Alicia, 16; Eddie, 18

This scene, again in the cafe, begins to establish Alicia and Eddie's mutual affection.

ALICIA: Are you doing homework?

EDDIE: No.

ALICIA: Can I see what you're writing?

EDDIE: It's in English.

ALICIA: Oh.

EDDIE: You wouldn't understand.

ALICIA: Is it a poem?

EDDIE: Sort of.

ALICIA: About me – sitting here in the moonlight, pensive and beautiful?

EDDIE: No.

ALICIA: Is it about your girlfriend back home with long golden hair and long golden legs?

EDDIE: I don't have a girlfriend.

ALICIA: Ahhh, Edmundo the priest.

EDDIE: When's your boyfriend coming for you?

ALICIA: In a month. The next new moon.

EDDIE: And he'll stay away from you that long?

ALICIA: He didn't like it. He pleaded with me. He swore he couldn't live without me. He cried. He raged like a bull. He said he'd cut me or he'd die if he didn't see me soon. But after all what's a couple more weeks.

EDDIE: It doesn't sound like you're in love with him. You're not that anxious to see him.

ALICIA: Well once you're married you know – you're married! That's it.

EDDIE: So don't get married.

ALICIA: I'm not like that. Once we run away together, we'll have to get married. That's the way it's done. Especially if your family disapproves of the match. After you've slept together – well everyone wants you married as soon as possible. The men get really mad. Machismo is nothing to fool around with. Men here are very jealous.

EDDIE: Men there too.

ALICIA: Really?

EDDIE: Yes.

ALICIA: I told my boyfriend about you.

EDDIE: Jesus Christ. Why?

ALICIA: To keep him in line.

EDDIE: Thanks a lot.

ALICIA: Can't you handle yourself?

EDDIE: I can handle myself and three others, if I have to.

ALICIA: Now you sound like one of us.

EDDIE: We're not so different.

ALICIA: Really?

EDDIE: Really.

ALICIA: Tell me – sometimes – don't you feel that when someone tells you not to do something – it's the very first thing you want to do?

EDDIE: Yeah. Sometimes.

ALICIA: Me too.

EDDIE: Don't play with me. I don't like it. (*Eddie continues writing.*)

ALICIA: Write about me. (*Eddie ignores her.*) You and I are taking Nyin to confession tomorrow. Did Chelo tell you?

EDDIE: She told me.

ALICIA: Will you confess everything?

EDDIE: I have nothing to confess.

ALICIA: I do. Good night.

EDDIE: Dream of angels –

ALICIA: So you dream of me. Write about Pipo. Why don't you?

Alicia, 16; Eddie, 18

In this final scene, Eddie catches up to Alicia near the river. Alicia has come here to be alone after an emotional argument with Eddie about their relationship. Mundo, a silent, lonely young man with mutant features, and a friend of Alicia and Eddie's, has also departed the dance, concerned for Alicia's well-being. When Eddie enters, Mundo is frightened off.

EDDIE: Alicia!

(*Mundo stands and leaves.*)

ALICIA: What?

EDDIE: He's here.

ALICIA: Miguel?

EDDIE: Yes.

ALICIA: Why did you follow me?

EDDIE: Are you kidding? I'd follow you to the end of the world.

ALICIA: Fool! Do you have a machete? A gun? This isn't a game.

EDDIE: What are you going to do? Let him come drag you away by the hair and fuck you so you have to get married. (*He grabs her.*) I could do that too.

ALICIA: (*Twisting away.*) You probably could.

EDDIE: You feel something for me. I know it.

ALICIA: Yes.

EDDIE: Don't go back. Stay here with me. (*He takes her hair in his hands.*) I'll stay here with you. I have to. I'm caught in your hair.

(*Kiss.*)

ALICIA: I never slept with him.

EDDIE: Shhhhh.

ALICIA: He's nineteen.

EDDIE: I don't want to hear.

ALICIA: I want you to hear. You should know.

EDDIE: No.

ALICIA: His name is Miguel. You have to know his name. He works in Poza Rica in the oil fields. He's thin. He comes to me after work, his shirt black with oil. His hands are rough and burned. We barely hold hands. We walk down the road and the back of our hands touch. That's enough. His house is one room with painted brick and he has a brand new stove. He'd tell me all about it. His life. He would share his whole life with me. And I know what kind of life it is. I would be his wife and stand in the mornings in a loose dress waving to him, the roof would be made of palm leaves and the floor cement. I could count on him and he could count on me. We know the same songs. He hardly smiles, but when he does – it's like the sun rising. He has an open smile. By what I'm doing – I'm closing it.

EDDIE: Stay with me. I want you so bad.

ALICIA: If I hurt him like this I can never go back. He'd spit on me and I'd deserve it.

EDDIE: Why would you have to go back? Do you love him?

ALICIA: How did this happen. A month ago I didn't know your
name.

EDDIE: I know.

ALICIA: And a month from now?

EDDIE: I'll make you forget everyone you ever knew.

(*They kiss.*)

Full Moon
By Reynolds Price

Kip, 21; Ora Lee, 22

Reynolds Price's *Full Moon* depicts the struggle between three young people to find purpose in life and to reconcile a relationship that entangles them. Set in rural North Carolina in the late 1930s, the story concerns Kerney Bascom, a young white girl; her boyfriend Kip Patrick, a white clerk, and Ora Lee Gaskin, the black daughter of Kip's maid, and Kip's frequent sexual partner. Kerney longs for a new and exciting life, away from the confines of small-town existence, while equally longing to marry Kip. However, Kip's inability to cut off his relationship with Ora Lee compounds Kerney's choice. Kip is steadfast in his desire to marry Kerney and yet cannot imagine a life that would totally exclude Ora Lee, who has been a friend and lover for many years. Ora Lee is resolved to get on with her life, without Kip. Eventually her plans are to take her young son (who no doubt, despite Ora's denial, was sired by Kip) north and start a new life. Within the struggle between the three young people, Kip and Kerney's fathers, and Ora Lee's mother, play a hand in pushing for resolution and marching into the future.

In the first scene, Kip has come to Ora's house with the intention of telling her that he cannot see her anymore. However, on seeing her, his desire returns.

◆ ◆ ◆

(*Ora runs out and stops short of Kip by several steps.*)
KIP: Thank the good Lord.
ORA: Hold your thanks till you see who I am.
KIP: I'd know you anywhere.
ORA: I don't know how. Seems like they used to call you Kipple Patrick.
KIP: (*His liquor shows in a shaky bow.*) At your service.
ORA: I don't need nothing you selling or giving.
KIP: I hope to be buying.
ORA: God, strike him dumb! I never took a penny –
KIP: Just a good many greenbacks, three or four rings, a locket with a curl of your best friend's hair, a pretty wristwatch – right many nice gifts down through the sweet years.
ORA: That gin don't smell too sweet – Kerney Bascomb's gin.

(*The sound of Kerney's name shocks and confuses Kip. He responds with a harshness that, though unnatural, begins to show him the awfulness of his purpose here.*)

KIP: (*Waits, grins.*) You put on some of your bleaching cream and go spying on the dance? Didn't see you there.

ORA: You ain't been seeing nothing dark as me these days.

KIP: My eyes can always find you.

(*Ora sees him at last with revulsion. She cannot speak yet but she mimes spitting at him.*)

KIP: (*Laughs.*) You knew our game.

ORA: *Game?* What kind of game – you telling me all I hope to hear, through all these years? Then just because Jeffer Burns saw the light on that Bascomb bitch, you take your face right out of here. Well, keep it gone. I'm thriving, sucker.

KIP: (*Stung but hiding it.*) I heard you were. Dave Robbins been seen riding out this way.

ORA: I been needing to tell you in person. Dave Robbins know the pathway to Paradise now.

KIP: Davey's all right, a safe old boy.

ORA: He take his time but he touch all bases.

KIP: (*Laughs.*) Whoa! Still, Dave's not all that strong in the head. (*Taps his forehead.*) Wrecks his car every week, bad judgment. (*Mock-whisper.*) Small brain –

ORA: You the big brain, sure. Everybody know Kip's right most days. Hell, you could dress me, ride me to Raleigh to the Governor's Mansion, say I was yours – me and my brown butt – and the Governor's wife would shake my hand and set me down like an actual lady that she couldn't smell.

KIP: It'd be fun to try.

ORA: Some other year. Ora's tired this year. Needs to head back to sleep.

KIP: That pains me to hear.

ORA: It'll pain you a heap-damned-worse if I stay. I'm too naked though to be in the night and too tired of you.

(*Ora turns toward the house.*)

KIP: Want to take a short ride?

(*Ora continues walking till she reaches the porch steps.*)

ORA: (*Mocking her own accent.*) I tell what's the truth, white man – Ora Lee's night-riding days are past.

KIP: What about Dave Robbins, his big green roadster?

ORA: That's a whole nother business – Dave drives me in *daylight*. (*She climbs the steps and stands on the stoop.*)

KIP: You going to say goodbye at least?

ORA: For a crisp new five-dollar bill, cash money.

KIP: Your words come high, lot higher than your –

ORA: Kipple, Kip – leave yourself *something* here.

KIP: Like what?

ORA: Not meanness, not trash.
(*Kip by now sees half the awfulness implicit in his being here at all, yet he cannot want to leave.*)

KIP: Could we start this over someway – do it right?

ORA: I didn't mean that. You too old, Kipple, to play this game. Too old and white – too white in the heart. God keeping score on your life now. Angels watching your hands. (*Kip looks at both hands.*) You go on home. (*Points.*) That road yonder, right past Kerney Bascomb's. Don't blow no horn now or wake her up. She need all the beauty sleep she can get; might help her dry little titties grow.

KIP: (*With controlled force.*) Keep that name out of your *mouth* forever.

ORA: (*Smiles.*) My mouth ain't dirty – didn't used to be.
(*Kip shuts his eyes and waits to calm. But his bafflement rises. He wipes his lips slowly with the back of a hand.*)

KIP: (*Nods his head firmly.*) Filthy – tonight.

ORA: (*Waits.*) Be nice now, son. Don't make bad blood. You be needing me – you and your poor daddy – when the nigger folks rise.

KIP: (*Smiles.*) They all eating yeast?

ORA: Oh no. Eating knives. Eating cold wind and rain.

KIP: Remember me then. I'll lean on you.

ORA: Don't lean too hard; I might not know you. Might hand you over to the first hungry child.

KIP: Throw your mind back – four summers ago, way deep in the trees. First time you showed me all your sweetness.

ORA: Seem like I'm forgetting right much these days.

KIP: But work on it, Ora. Next time we'll find out what we got left.

ORA: Next time I'll be too bright for you to see. I'm getting more splendid by the night now, boy. Be good to your eyes; don't glance at Ora – her and her son and all her kin. She'll blind you fast.

(She launches a final dazzling smile, then slowly goes in. Kip stands a moment, fixing the memory. Then he shakes his head in confusion and leaves.)

◆ ◆ ◆ ◆

Kip, 21; Ora Lee, 22

In this scene, Kip comes to Ora's house to try to make up for the trouble over these last few weeks.

Kip climbs the steps of Sarah's house and knocks once. No answer. He knocks again louder.

KIP: Ora Lee. Please. *(More silence.)* Lawrence? You in there? This is Kipple Patrick, your mother's friend.

(Kip takes the jewel bag from his pocket and tries the door. It opens wide – on Ora standing far back, dressed for church. She is bolt upright, arms at her sides; and she stares past Kip. Their meeting unfolds with a measured slowness – no frantic haste but calm deliberation from both.)

KIP: Ora – I'm sorry. I was going to leave this. *(Extends the bag.)* *(Ora shakes her head No, slowly.)*
Sell it then; put the money on Lawrence.

ORA: Lawrence got all the money he need.

KIP: Then he must not need what children need –

ORA: Lawrence growing the way his bones *want* to grow – his bones and his good mother's mind. *(Presses a finger against her brow.)* Look in here, Kip.

KIP: But when he starts to school and all, the day might come –

ORA: The day might come when God in the sky want to punish you.

(*She turns back, finds her purse and parasol. Then she advances on Kip and holds the door as if to shut it behind her.*)

KIP: You going to late church?

ORA: I'm going anywhere I want to.

(*She walks out, shuts the door and locks it with a key. When she has passed Kip and stopped in the yard, she opens the parasol. Kip stays on the porch.*)

KIP: Don't get sunburned.

ORA: (*Lowering the parasol.*) Might as well burn now and save on later. I don't want to fry in Hell next to you. (*Begins to leave.*)

KIP: This hurts a whole lot worse than I planned.

ORA: It don't hurt me.

KIP: Sarah said different.

ORA: My mother is an old-*timey* soul. She thinks everybody keeping score like her, all the time losing and moaning about it.

KIP: And you're modernistic?

ORA: Call it that if it helps you out. I told you last night – I'm moving, white man. Every part of this body you see is working and sweet, Kip, *sweet.*

KIP: When you say my name, it still sounds sweet.

ORA: Better take your ears to the doctor then.

(*Kip laughs a short note, then tries to step toward her. Ora holds up a silent hand to balk him.*)

KIP: Where's Lawrence now?

ORA: Why you hollering on about Lawrence? You barely mentioned his name before. That child is mine.

KIP: Could I see him a minute?

ORA: If you got X-ray eyes you could. He in Sunday School. Don't you go near him – embarrass him to death. (*Turns to leave.*)

KIP: What if I touch you – touch, just touch?

ORA: Everywhere you press, my skin would bruise.

KIP: Was it really that bad?

ORA: Not bad a bit. We were children, Kip. Now we tigers and lions.

KIP: (*Half-smiles.*) You're the tiger, God knows.

ORA: And the tiger's *leaving*.

KIP: Heading up north? Mighty cold up there.

ORA: Cold down *here,* depending on your house. But ease your mind. I won't be sending you no postcards for Kerney to read.

KIP: Let's leave her out. We can live without her.

ORA: You asking me can you live with her and still bump me? (*One low note of laughter.*)

KIP: (*Waits.*) Is it cruel as it sounds?

ORA: A lot you do seem to turn out cruel. (*Waits.*) No skin off me; I told you I'm leaving.

KIP: Will Lawrence stay?

ORA: Talk to your brain, Kip; it's seriously dumb. You ain't got a particle of right to that child.

KIP: So I tell you goodbye?

ORA: (*Meets his eyes and waits a long moment.*) For the ten-thousandth time – goodbye, thank *Jesus*.
(*Ora gracefully leaves in languorous strides. Kip waits a moment, goes to the door and sets the jewel bag down on the sill. Then he leaves too.*)

Hey, There – Hello!
By Gennadi Mamlin; Translated by Miriam Morton

Masha, 14; Valerka, 15

Hey, There – Hello! is the story of two Russian teenagers, Masha and Valerka, who live next door to one another. First produced in Moscow in 1969, this play mixes fantasy with reality as it explores the struggles and emotions and beliefs and insecurities of its young protagonists. In the scene below Valerka, whose family performs a variety act, has just been encouraging Masha to join their show since she is, as he says, "a one-woman circus."

Masha says she wouldn't dare because her grandmother, with whom she lives, despises all show people. Masha has brought Valerka a picnic lunch of lemonade and sandwiches; they sit and Valerka takes up the food hungrily.

VALERKA: Is today Sunday?

MASHA: Today? No, it's Wednesday.

VALERKA: Then why did you dress up this morning?

MASHA: I didn't dress up. This is an ordinary blouse. And my good shoes – that's all. Why – do I look that way?

VALERKA: Which way?

MASHA: Festive. "Which way!!"

VALERKA: You look silly. The blouse is too big.

MASHA: I'll grow into it. In another six months it will fit just right.

VALERKA: Then why don't you wait half a year to wear it? And what a mess your hair is! You look like a scarecrow. (*Masha snatches the lemonade bottle from his hand and is about to throw it into the sea.*) Hey! Hey! Can't you take a joke? (*Masha lowers her arm.*) Actually it's a cute hairdo. (*He takes back his bottle and drinks.*)

MASHA: (*Looks down at her blouse.*) Maybe it *is* too garish.

VALERKA: (*Continues to eat with gusto.*) It's not important. You should care! (*Masha takes off her blouse.*) That's different. What's important is not to be on display, not to pose as a grande dame, to be your age. You may wear eye makeup that makes you look like an aging woman, but, just the same, you'll be running on the beach like a kid.

MASHA: "Not to be on display," you say. But you yourself wear patches on your pants.

VALERKA: Jeans. They are practical. The "patch" is a trademark. I had sewn it on myself then you'd have the right to call me a fop. Do you know what I mean?

MASHA: No.

VALERKA: It's the same thing whether you decorate your jeans or let your hair grow down to your knees. It's all the same thing – you're trying to attract attention to stand out. Do you want some of this? (*Offers her the lemonade bottle.*)

MASHA: Okay. (*Takes a couple of swallows from the bottle.*) It's interesting – first you drink, now I do . . . Don't you see? The same bottle – the same source. Look: I took a sip, and now (*Offering him the bottle.*) you'll drink from the very same bottle!

VALERKA: (*Finally getting what she's driving at.*) You'd better forget about your idiotic dates. I think they were disgusting. (*He examines the sandwich.*) I've never seen such red bacon.

MASHA: My grandmother hoarded some. And while she was quarreling with one of her tenants, I sneaked down the cellar and grabbed a piece.

VALERKA: (*Gets his back up.*) I've made it! I've arrived! I'm now consuming stolen goods!

MASHA: (*Insulted.*) Be careful how you talk. It's one thing to steal – another to take secretly. Bacon is bacon – isn't it all the same to you?

VALERKA: (*Shouts with exasperation.*) You're a wooden dummy – with eyes – that's what you are! Everything is "all the same" to you. But I'm not used to sneaking things. I don't do it myself and I hate it when it's done for my sake. It degrades me. Can you understand that?

MASHA: No, I can't. When you anonymously write down a complaint against a fellow-student in the class book, don't you, in a way, shout it all over the school?

VALERKA: What a comparison! The class book is about the way people act toward one another. (*He is about to take another bite of the sandwich, stops, and then throws it into the sea.*)

MASHA: (*Takes the bottle, looks through it into the light, pours out the rest of the lemonade, and sings in a low voice.*)
"Oh, why did you, that Monday,
Give me a white rose . . . "

VALERKA: All right, don't sulk . . . My uncle – that's my mother's cousin – has a philosophy of life something like yours. Last night I looked into his room through the window. He sits there eating candy. He had kept it under his pillow, and now sat there chewing away. Never a thought about sharing it. That's why I left the house earlier this morning. I couldn't stand to look at him. What if he had noticed that I caught him at his secret feasting? . . . In general he's a unique type. I moved into the shed and gave him my room. He had been upset because some of our tenants had rooms facing the sea and he didn't. "I," he said, "am your mother's cousin. If you don't have a feeling of kinship for me, I might just as well live with strangers."

MASHA: And who is he? What does he do?

VALERKA: It's hard to tell. He hints about having an important position. He is about to retire on a pension. Wants to buy a little house in our town. That guy won't miss a chance to rake in the rubles. Ever since I can remember, we never locked our door. But that one, even when he goes to the store for a bottle of soda, he latches his window and locks the door to his room.

MASHA: Maybe he brought a lot of cash with him.

VALERKA: Or maybe diamonds! And of course I'd steal them! I, or Guido, or Nikolai. (*Suddenly he becomes aware that Masha has put her head on his shoulder.*) So you found yourself a pillow? (*He shakes her off.*) You're weird! We're right here at the beach – it's full of people who know us. Do you want our names to be written on all the fences with the immortal words: "Tantamount to love . . . ?"

MASHA: Let them!

VALERKA: (*Jumps up.*) Of course you wouldn't care! You're shameless!

MASHA: (*Slyly.*) Valerka, what's that you have in your pocket?

VALERKA: (*Perplexed.*) Nothing.

MASHA: And you claim to be truthful! You have some tickets there. For the movie, "Green Mansions." Slavka*, the postoffice clerk, told me that you bought them for yourself and Vera. That's what you've got there, isn't it?

VALERKA: (*Still feigning perplexity.*) Of course, since you say that I bought them – that's how it must be. (*He takes the tickets from his pocket.*)

MASHA: (*Snatches the tickets from his hand, stuffs them into her mouth, chews them up, and swallows them.*) There!

VALERKA: (*Extremely surprised.*) What a maniac! Using woodpulp for food!

MASHA: (*Taking some coins from her change purse.*) Here, you can give Vera her money back.

VALERKA: (*Knocks the coins from her hand.*) Oh! – get lost! . . . Vanish, I tell you!
(*She begins to retreat and he calls after her.*)
Drop dead! (*Masha stops short.*) What's the matter with you? Have you gone and fallen in love with me?

MASHA: (*In an awkward pose.*) That's all I need – to fall in love with an idiot like you!

VALERKA: Just remember – I'm through with all of you women. As for you, don't disappoint me – drop dead!

MASHA: (*Now composed.*) Go ahead, be rude to me. Before, it would have bothered me, but now I couldn't care less. Now I see all your tricks as through a prism – that's how.

VALERKA: Through a what?

MASHA: Through a prism. It's like a scientific formula. If you're tired of talking nasty then why don't you pull my braids? This approach is also mentioned. Boys are known to hide their feelings that way. (*She takes a pamphlet from her shopping*

*SLAVka – The a's pronounced as in arm.

bag and reads its title.) "The Awkward Age, or Reaching Manhood" by Khmelnitzkii*, who wrote it especially for creatures your age. Read it. It says it right here about hiding feelings. (*Shows him page in book.*)

VALERKA: (*With curiosity, reading.*) "At the age of 16, sometimes a little earlier, sometimes later . . . "

MASHA: (*Reads on.*) " . . . you begin to notice girls. You are a bit ashamed as to these stirrings of interest in them, and hide it from your friends . . . " (*Continues reading – louder.*) " . . . And when you are attracted to a certain girl, you try to appear cross with her, rude and curt." There – clear enough – black on white. They sell it at the newspaper stand. (*She walks away a safe distance and declaims rhapsodically.*) "When a certain girl attracts you . . . "

VALERKA: Just listen to her. You'd think she was memorizing a prayer.

MASHA: (*Triumphantly.*) " . . . you try to be cross, rude, curt . . . "

VALERKA: How disgusting!

MASHA: That's right, go on – spit at me. Reach manhood!

VALERKA: (*He jumps at Masha, grabs the pamphlet, and hurls it into the sea.*) One more word out of you and you'll be next!

MASHA: (*With the unctuousness of a martyr to the truth.*) You cannot drown the truth. (*Valerka pushes Masha into the water. She falls with a big splash.*)

---

* *KhmelNITZkii – Pronounced with the e as in net, and the ii as in meet.*

I Never Saw Another Butterfly
By Celeste Raspanti

Honza, 16; Raja, 16

I Never Saw Another Butterfly depicts the plight of young Jewish children who were held in a ghetto at Terezin, a military garrison set up by the Nazis as a stopping off place for hundreds of thousands being sent to Auschwitz for extermination in the gas chambers. Of the 15,000 children at Terezin, only about 100 survived. One girl, Raja Englanderova, lived to return to her home in Prague. Using actual journals, diaries, letters, poems, drawings and pictures by the children of Terezin as its source material, this play imaginatively recreates the life of Raja, who gave hope to children around her.

In the first scene below, a transport train crowded and boarded up has just departed for Auschwitz. Raja, whose brother and new bride have been taken away, turns to discover Honza, a young man who has just lost his brother.

HONZA: (*Staring after the train.*) Jiri – they said they wouldn't take him. He was a plumber, an electrician – so clever – they said they wouldn't take him . . .

RAJA: Everyone goes . . . Jiri? Was he your friend?

HONZA: (*Turning.*) He was my brother . . .

RAJA: You're Honza Kosek. I heard about you. My name is Raja – Raja Englanderova. My brother . . . Pavel . . . and Irca . . .

HONZA: I know . . . they got married, and they're on the train now . . . what's the good of that?

RAJA: (*Turning away, a little angry.*) They're still together.

HONZA: What's the good of that!

RAJA: Together they'll not be afraid. That's the good!

HONZA: (*Embarrassed.*) *You* are afraid.

RAJA: What if I am? You're laughing at me . . . you think I'm a coward . . .

HONZA: I'm laughing at you because you're a girl, and don't know the first thing about – about anything.

RAJA: Well . . . it's all easy for you. I've heard how you get by the guards – it's easy for a boy.

Honza: Maybe. (*He touches her shoulder almost tenderly and turns her around to face him.*) My father was beaten and left for dead before my eyes. I saw it. I couldn't move, I was so afraid. But I didn't run. I never understood it – until my father dying told me, "You're a good boy, Honza; you are afraid, but you are not a coward."

Raja: (*Ashamed.*) I'm sorry . . . (*Reluctantly.*) Well, it's late . . . I have to go . . .

Honza: Where're you going?

Raja: Number twenty-five . . . Where do you live?

Honza: House number two – on the other side, near the wall.

Raja: (*Eager to talk.*) There're thirty girls – in our group – most of us from Prague . . . Irena . . . she's in charge of the whole compound – she lives with us.

Honza: We live alone; we elect our own leader – and we have meetings – secret ones.

Raja: Don't you have one of the older men there?

Honza: What for? We're all old enough – we work in the fields.

Raja: So do we – some of us. I do. I'm old enough.

Honza: We take care of everything ourselves. I'm the leader now – I was elected. So I'm in charge.

Raja: Don't you go to school – at night, after work?

Honza: We do – sometimes. Sometimes we have meetings – the leaders from the boys' homes – and we talk and plan.

Raja: What?

Honza: Oh, like someone gets an idea about something and we talk about it – or someone does something we don't like and we tell him to quit it or else. A lot of things. We're working on something right now.

Raja: For the boys' home?

Honza: Well, not just for the boys – we're going to have a newspaper and report the news in camp.

Raja: Have you got a printing press?

Honza: No – we don't need that. It's not that kind of paper. We make copies of the news and hang them around in the barracks. It's my idea . . .

RAJA: Will you put one in the girls' home?

HONZA: I suppose we could – I never thought about it.

RAJA: I'd copy it over – I could do that.

HONZA: I'd have to talk about it with the rest. I suppose it's a good idea . . . Well, I guess I've got to go now – we're going to have a meeting about the paper. (*He walks away, and then turns, shrugging a shoulder at her.*) You can come if you want to. (*She hesitates, and then runs to him.*)
(*Lights go down as Raja walks downstage, speaking to the audience.*)

RAJA: And so *Vedem* was born – and lived for three years, and helped us live. We waited to read the copy posted in our barracks, and later when, for safety, it was read aloud, no one was missing. It was an invisible line of communication between the houses so that even across the dark yards and crowded barracks, the youth of Terezin grew up together.

HONZA: (*Calling form the darkness to Raja, who has just finished speaking.*) Raja? (*Lights up on the area when she enters.*)

RAJA: Yes? I can only stay a few minutes. Is this week's *Vedem* ready?

HONZA: Here it is . . .

RAJA: I'll take it and get started. (*She turns.*)

HONZA: Wait . . . I was thinking . . . We've talked about it at the meeting . . . we could run some of the poems from the girls' house – when there's room.

RAJA: Good. Irena will be glad of that. She said it might happen. The smaller girls got all excited!

HONZA: There won't be room for too many . . .

RAJA: I'll tell her. (*She turns to leave, almost reluctantly.*) I'll see you . . .

HONZA: Wait . . . I saw you in the field today. Of course I couldn't say anything.

RAJA: I know. I saw you – across the road.

HONZA: Maybe we could plan a way to meet there – in case . . . there are messages . . . or anything.

RAJA: It wouldn't be safe! The guards are everywhere.

HONZA: We meet here . . . at night.

RAJA: The guards think we're inside the barracks.

HONZA: I'm not afraid . . . are you?

RAJA: No . . . yes, I guess I am. They'd beat you.

HONZA: It wouldn't be the first time. I always get up again . . .

RAJA: Some day . . .

HONZA: Some day, maybe, I won't, I suppose. What difference does it make?

RAJA: Don't talk like that. I'll go if you do. (*Starts to leave.*)

HONZA: Wait . . . wait. I'm only teasing.

RAJA: It would be lonesome without you. I mean, the boys need you, and the paper. Irena says you're the only one she can trust to bury the drawings and poems.

HONZA: Others would do that . . .

RAJA: It would be hard . . . I mean . . . these months we've been good friends . . . I'd miss you, too. (*She walks over to his side.*)

HONZA: (*After a silence; taking her hand.*) I meant to say that first.

RAJA: I know. (*They walk together in silence, hand in hand, to the edge of the lighted area.*) Good night . . .

HONZA: Good night. (*They separate and run to other lighted areas. Turning away, they speak to each other across the darkness.*) Raja, Raja!

RAJA: Yes . . .

HONZA: I have some flowers for you.

RAJA: Honza, if you get caught . . .

HONZA: You know the square in front of the tower . . .

RAJA: The prisoners aren't allowed there . . .

HONZA: I know, but they can't stop us from looking at it. Look, from here . . . see the flowers near the corner – and the butterflies? . . .

RAJA: I see them . . .

HONZA: Well, I'm giving them to you, and every time you pass . . .

RAJA: I'll say – they're mine. Honza gave them to me – all the flowers – and all the butterflies. Thank you, oh, thank you . . . (*They turn into another lighted area.*) Honza, Irena gave me a book of poetry – I left it for you at the end of the field near the shed. I want you to read one special poem . . .

HONZA: I found it – and read it – and left one for you . . . look for it. (*They hold hands and run together into another area.*) Raja, look . . .

RAJA: (*Holding a small package.*) What is it?

HONZA: Open it – careful – it's very expensive.

RAJA: It must be – since you crawled through the barracks to bring it. Why didn't you leave it in the shed?

HONZA: It can't be left – not around here.

RAJA: (*Opening package slowly, pulling out a sausage.*) Honza, a sausage – you're wonderful – and sausage, I haven't – but where did you get it?

HONZA: I liberated it . . .

RAJA: Liberated it? Honza . . .

HONZA: Actually, I took it.

RAJA: (*Biting one end, then handing him the other.*) Stole it. No wonder it tastes so good – you're so brave! (*They hold hands and run together to another area.*)

HONZA: (*Haltingly.*) I won't be here – for a few days . . .

RAJA: Why? Where are you going?

HONZA: Don't take any chances – coming to meet me, I mean.

RAJA: (*Frightened.*) Honza, what is it?

HONZA: Nothing. A special detail to build something outside the fortifications. They're picking the strongest – I'll be chosen.

RAJA: But – what if something happens?

HONZA: There'll be a chance for extra food. (*Smiles.*) Maybe another sausage.

RAJA: I don't care about the sausage . . . Honza, I'm afraid!

HONZA: Don't worry . . . they want the job done – it's some kind of walled courtyard . . . nothing much can happen . . . Well, I have to go.

RAJA: (*Reluctantly, almost angrily.*) Good-bye then . . . (*They walk together to the edge of the lighted area. Honza walks into the darkness.*) Good-bye. I'll be waiting . . . waiting . . . Please come back. (*She sits with her head in her hands.*)

In this scene, a wall separates Raja from Honza, who is about to be transported to Auschwitz.

Lights come up on Raja, seated. She seems wounded and stunned by the names she hears. When she hears Honza's name, she runs to the edge of the lighted area, searching the darkness. Honza can be heard, but not seen.

RAJA: Honza?

HONZA: Raja . . . don't – don't turn or move.

RAJA: (*Trying to locate the voice.*) Honza, where are you?

HONZA: Don't move. Here, on the other side of the wall – don't move, don't – just listen. I have a number in this transport.

RAJA: No! (*She searches in the darkness for him, moving on hands and knees.*)

HONZA: Please – don't turn, don't move . . . I have a number . . . I must report . . .

RAJA: No!

HONZA: But the news is good . . .

RAJA: What do you mean?

HONZA: The war is coming to an end . . .

RAJA: Honza . . . no!

HONZA: Things are going bad for the Nazis – something will happen before long . . . Raja, please, listen . . .

RAJA: Honza . . . where are you . . . I'm coming with you.

HONZA: You can't . . . it's too late. You must wait here.

RAJA: (*Quieter, but intensely.*) I cannot . . . Where are you?

HONZA: No . . . you must wait . . .for me.

RAJA: (*Angrily.*) Honza, I cannot live waiting . . . Please, please, where are you, where are you . . . (*Pleading with him.*)

HONZA: (*Tenderly.*) I am with you – wherever you are . . . Listen, Raja . . .

RAJA: (*Vanquished.*) I'm listening. (*She stares unseeing into the darkness.*)

HONZA: I have something. I never told you – about the poem. I wrote one, too, for the contest, remember?

RAJA: (*Dazedly.*) You never handed it in . . .

HONZA: It was supposed to be about a memory, only it's about you . . .

RAJA: You never told me . . .

HONZA: I'll leave it here, under the post near the corner. Read it some time . . . but . . . don't laugh . . . you laughed once at the other poem, remember?

RAJA: I remember.

HONZA: When you read this . . .

RAJA: I won't laugh . . . I won't. I promise . . . Honza . . . (*She starts to move toward the darkness.*)

HONZA: Don't, don't, don't come out here. The guards . . . Just stay there, stay there, and wait. Good-bye . . . (*He leaves.*)

RAJA: Honza . . . Honza? . . . Good-bye . . .

(*She walks to the edge of the area and finds the sheet of paper. She reads, and Honza's voice is heard reading with her.*)

Memory, come tell a fairy tale
About my girl who's lost and gone.
Tell, tell about the golden grail
And bid the swallow, bring her back to me.

Fly close to her and ask her soft and low
If she thinks of me sometimes with love,
If she is well? Ask too before you go
If I am still her dearest, precious dove.
And hurry back, don't lose your way.
So I can think of other things.

(*Raja stops reading and Honza's voice continues.*)

HONZA: But you were too lovely, perhaps, to stay.

I loved you once. Good-bye, my love.

RAJA: (*Folding the paper very slowly, carefully.*) Good-bye. It was the motto of Terezin. It should have been written over the entrance instead of the lie that greeted newcomers: "Work makes us free." It was *good-bye*, not *work*, that made us free. It was the only thing we knew would never change. Good-bye

. . . good-bye . . . good-bye. It freed us all. What was there to fear when you had said good-bye to everyone you ever loved?

Joe Turner's Come and Gone
By August Wilson

Zonia, 11; Reuben, 11

Pulitzer Prize-winning author August Wilson sets this play in Pittsburgh in 1911. In a black boardinghouse, owned and operated by Seth and Bertha Holly, a collection of black characters form the fabric of the story in which the past and the present collide. The struggle of black Americans to become a part of the industrial age is tested by the spiritual and mystical heritage of a culture leaving the pain of slavery behind. Among the players in the Holly boardinghouse is Herald Loomis, recently arrived with his young daughter, Zonia, in search of his wife. An air of mystery surrounds Loomis, whose daughter struggles to understand their mission amidst the many stops their journey has taken.

In the first scene, Zonia is in the Holly yard, where she meets young Reuben (a local boy) for the first time.

Reuben enters.

REUBEN: Hi.

ZONIA: Hi.

REUBEN: What's your name?

ZONIA: Zonia.

REUBEN: What kind of name is that?

ZONIA: It's what my daddy named me.

REUBEN: My name's Reuben. You staying in Mr. Seth's house?

ZONIA: Yeah.

REUBEN: That your daddy I seen you with this morning?

ZONIA: I don't know. Who you see me with?

REUBEN: I saw you with some man had on a great big old coat. And you was walking up to Mr. Seth's house. Had on a hat too.

ZONIA: Yeah, that's my daddy.

REUBEN: You like Mr. Seth?

ZONIA: I ain't see him much.

REUBEN: My grandpap say he a great big old windbag. How come you living in Mr. Seth's house? Don't you have no house?

ZONIA: We going to find my mother.

REUBEN: Where she at?

ZONIA: I don't know. We got to find her. We just go all over.

REUBEN: Why you got to find her? What happened to her?

ZONIA: She ran away.

REUBEN: Why she run away?

ZONIA: I don't know. My daddy say some man named Joe Turner
   did something bad to him once and that made her run away.

REUBEN: Maybe she coming back and you don't have to go looking
   for her.

ZONIA: We ain't there no more.

REUBEN: She could have come back when you wasn't there.

ZONIA: My daddy said she ran off and left us so we going looking
   for her.

REUBEN: What he gonna do when he find her?

ZONIA: He didn't say. He just say he got to find her.

REUBEN: Your daddy say how long you staying in Mr. Seth's house?

ZONIA: He don't say much. But we never stay too long nowhere. He
   say we got to keep moving till we find her.

REUBEN: Ain't no kids hardly live around here. I had me a friend but
   he died. He was the best friend I ever had. Me and Eugene
   used to keep secrets. I still got his pigeons. He told me to let
   them go when he died. He say, "Reuben, promise me when I
   die you'll let my pigeons go." But I keep them to remember
   him by. I ain't never gonna let them go. Even when I get to be
   grown up. I'm just always gonna have Eugene's pigeons.
   (Pause.)
   Mr. Bynum a conjure man. My grandpap scared of him. He
   don't like me to come over here too much. I'm scared of him
   too. My grandpap told me not to let him get close enough to
   where he can reach out his hand and touch me.

ZONIA: He don't seem scary to me.

REUBEN: He buys pigeons from me . . . and if you get up early in the
   morning you can see him out in the yard doing something
   with them pigeons. My grandpap say he kill them. I sold him
   one yesterday. I don't know what he do with it. I just hope he

don't spook me up.

ZONIA: Why you sell him pigeons if he's gonna spook you up?

REUBEN: I just do like Eugene do. He used to sell Mr. Bynum pigeons. That's how he got to collecting them to sell to Bynum. Sometime he give me a nickel and sometime he give me a whole dime.

(*Loomis enters from the house.*)

[LOOMIS: Zonia!]

[ZONIA: Sir?]

[LOOMIS: What you doing?]

[ZONIA: Nothing.]

[LOOMIS: You stay around this house, you hear? I don't want you wandering off nowhere.]

[ZONIA: I ain't wandering off nowhere.]

[LOOMIS: Miss Bertha set that hot tub and you getting a good scrubbing. Get scrubbed up good. You ain't been scrubbing.]

[ZONIA: I been scrubbing.]

[LOOMIS: Look at you. You growing too fast. Your bones getting bigger everyday. I don't want you getting grown on me. Don't you get grown on me too soon. We gonna find your mama. She around here somewhere. I can smell her. You stay on around this house now. Don't you go nowhere.]

[ZONIA: Yes, sir.]

(*Loomis exits into the house.*)

REUBEN: Wow, your daddy's scary!

ZONIA: He is not! I don't know what you talking about.

REUBEN: He got them mean-looking eyes!

ZONIA: My daddy ain't got no mean-looking eyes!

REUBEN: Aw, girl, I was just messing with you. You wanna go see Eugene's pigeons? Got a great big coop out the back of my house. Come on, I'll show you.

(*Reuben and Zonia exit as the lights go down.*)

Zonia, 11; Reuben, 11

In the next scene, again a meeting between Reuben and Zonia, Reuben recounts the strange events that took place the previous evening.

It is early the next morning. The lights come up on Zonia and Reuben in the yard.

REUBEN: Something spookly going on around here. Last night Mr. Bynum was out in the yard singing and talking to the wind . . . and the wind it just be talking back to him. Did you hear it?

ZONIA: I heard it. I was scared to get up and look. I thought it was a storm.

REUBEN: That wasn't no storm. That was Mr. Bynum. First he say something . . . and the wind it say back to him.

ZONIA: I heard it. Was you scared? I was scared.

REUBEN: And then this morning . . . I seen Miss Mabel!

ZONIA: Who Miss Mabel?

REUBEN: Mr. Seth's mother. He got her picture hanging up in the house. She been dead.

ZONIA: How you seen her if she been dead?

REUBEN: Zonia . . . if I tell you something you promise you won't tell anybody?

ZONIA: I promise.

REUBEN: It was early this morning . . . I went out to the coop to feed the pigeons. I was down on the ground like this to open up the door to the coop . . . when all of a sudden I seen some feets in front of me. I looked up . . . and there was Miss Mabel standing there.

ZONIA: Reuben, you better stop telling that! You ain't seen nobody!

REUBEN: Naw, it's the truth. I swear! I seen her just like I see you. Look . . . you can see where she hit me with her cane.

ZONIA: Hit you? What she hit you for?

REUBEN: She says, "Didn't you promise Eugene something?" Then she hit me with her cane. She say, "Let them pigeons go." Then she hit me again. That's what made them marks.

ZONIA: Jeez man . . . get away from me. You done see a haunt!

REUBEN: Shhhh. You promised, Zonia!

ZONIA: You sure it wasn't Miss Bertha come over there and hit you
with her hoe?

REUBEN: It wasn't no Miss Bertha. I told you it was Miss Mabel. She
was standing right there by the coop. She had this light
coming out of her and then she just melted away.

ZONIA: What she had on?

REUBEN: A white dress. Ain't even had no shoes or nothing. Just
had on that white dress and them big hands . . . and that cane
she hit me with.

ZONIA: How you reckon she knew about the pigeons? You reckon
Eugene told her?

REUBEN: I don't know. I sure ain't asked her none. She say Eugene
was waiting on them pigeons. Say he couldn't go back home
till I let them go. I couldn't get the door to the coop open fast
enough.

ZONIA: Maybe she an angel? From the way you say she look with
that white dress. Maybe she an angel.

REUBEN: Mean as she was . . . how she gonna be an angel? She
used to chase us out her yard and frown up and look evil all
the time.

ZONIA: That don't mean she can't be no angel 'cause of how she
looked and 'cause she wouldn't let no kids play in her yard. It
go by if you got any spots on your heart and if you pray and
go to church.

REUBEN: What about she hit me with her cane? An angel wouldn't
hit me with her cane.

ZONIA: I don't know. She might. I still say she was an angel.

REUBEN: You reckon Eugene the one who sent old Miss Mabel?

ZONIA: Why he send her? Why don't he come himself?

REUBEN: Figured if he send her maybe that'll make me listen. 'Cause
she old.

ZONIA: What you think it feel like?

REUBEN: What?

ZONIA: Being dead.

REUBEN: Like being sleep only you don't know nothing and can't move no more.

ZONIA: If Miss Mabel can come back . . . then maybe Eugene can come back too.

REUBEN: We can go down to the hideout like we used to! He could come back everyday! It be just like he ain't dead.

ZONIA: Maybe that ain't right for him to come back. Feel kinda funny to be playing games with a haunt.

REUBEN: Yeah . . . what if everybody came back? What if Miss Mabel came back just like she ain't dead? Where you and your daddy gonna sleep then?

ZONIA: Maybe they go back at night and don't need no place to sleep.

REUBEN: It still don't seem right. I'm sure gonna miss Eugene. He's the bestest friend anybody ever had.

ZONIA: My daddy say if you miss somebody too much it can kill you. Say he missed me till it liked to kill him.

REUBEN: What if your mama's already dead and all the time you looking for her?

ZONIA: Naw, she ain't dead. My daddy say he can smell her.

REUBEN: You can't smell nobody that ain't here. Maybe he smelling old Miss Bertha. Maybe Miss Bertha your mama?

ZONIA: Naw, she ain't. My mamma got long pretty hair and she five feet from the ground!

REUBEN: Your daddy say when you leaving? (*Zonia doesn't respond.*) Maybe you gonna stay in Mr. Seth's house and don't go looking for your mama no more.

ZONIA: He say we got to leave on Saturday.

REUBEN: Dag! You just only been here for a little while. Don't seem like nothing ever stay the same.

ZONIA: He say he got to find her. Find him a place in the world.

REUBEN: He could find him a place in Mr. Seth's house.

ZONIA: It don't look like we never gonna find her.

REUBEN: Maybe he find her by Saturday then you don't have to go.

ZONIA: I don't know.

REUBEN: You look like a spider!

ZONIA: I ain't no spider!

REUBEN: Got them long skinny arms and legs. You look like one of them Black Widows.

ZONIA: I ain't no Black Widow nothing! My name is Zonia!

REUBEN: That's what I'm gonna call you . . . Spider.

ZONIA: You can call me that, but I don't have to answer.

REUBEN: You know what? I think maybe I be your husband when I grow up.

ZONIA: How you know?

REUBEN: I ask my grandpap how you know and he say when the moon falls into a girl's eyes that how you know.

ZONIA: Did it fall into my eyes?

REUBEN: Not that I can tell. Maybe I ain't old enough. Maybe you ain't old enough.

ZONIA: So there! I don't know why you telling me that lie!

REUBEN: That don't mean nothing 'cause I can't see it. I know it's there. Just the way you look at me sometimes look like the moon might have been in your eyes.

ZONIA: That don't mean nothing if you can't see it. You supposed to see it.

REUBEN: Shucks, I see it good enough for me. You ever let anybody kiss you?

ZONIA: Just my daddy. He kiss me on the cheek.

REUBEN: It's better on the lips. Can I kiss you on the lips?

ZONIA: I don't know. You ever kiss anybody before?

REUBEN: I had a cousin let me kiss her on the lips one time. Can I kiss you?

ZONIA: Okay. (*Reuben kisses her and lays his head against her chest.*) What you doing?

REUBEN: Listening. Your heart singing!

ZONIA: It is not.

REUBEN: Just beating like a drum. Let's kiss again. (*They kiss again.*) Now you mine, Spider. You my girl, okay?

ZONIA: Okay.

REUBEN: When I get grown, I come looking for you.

ZONIA: Okay.

(*The lights fade to black.*)

The Less Than Human Club
By Timothy Mason

Clinton, 17; Melissa, 14

Set in Minneapolis in 1967 and 1968, *The Less Than Human Club* concerns the lives of eight teenagers during a year that was turbulent both personally and historically. The central character, Davis, sets the play in context at the beginning. When we first see Davis, he is in his thirties. His need to resolve conflicts set up in his Junior year in high school takes us back to that important year. The play deals with themes of deception, race relations, integrity, and designs and hopes for a future. Before the flashback year is over, Davis is given an insight that stings as it resolves.

In this first scene, Clinton, a young black man in conflict with his conservative parents and his own beliefs, practices a speech by Martin Luther King, Jr. He is then joined by his sister, Melissa, who shares her frustrations about the strict demands made by their parents.

Maybe there's a spot on Clinton. He stands at the microphone. Under this we hear the trumpet: "Leaning on the Everlasting Arm."

CLINTON: "I know you are asking today, How long will it take? I come to say to you this afternoon, however difficult the moment, however frustrating the hour, it will not be long, because truth pressed to earth will rise again.

"How long? Not long, because no lie can live forever.

"How long? Not long, because you still reap what you sow.

"How long? Not long. Because the arm of the moral universe is long, but it bends toward justice.

"How long? Not long. 'Cause mine eyes have seen the glory of the coming of the Lord . . . He has sounded forth the trumpets that shall never call retreat. He is lifting up the hearts of man before His judgment seat. Oh, be swift, my soul, to answer Him. Be jubilant, my feet. Our God is marching on."
(We hear a vast audience responding – shouting – applauding. Melissa enters.)

MELISSA: I'm sick of it.

CLINTON: Hey! Respect.

MELISSA: They push and they push. What do they want from us?

CLINTON: You gotta ask?

MELISSA: Don't tell me you don't feel it. You bring home straight A's, anybody else's folks be so happy, they buy you a car. But no . . .

CLINTON: Shut up now.

MELISSA: "Did you earn this, or did you get it by charm." I'm sick of it!

CLINTON: They're just, you know, doing the best they can.

MELISSA: So am I, dammit! Clinton, it's Homecoming.

CLINTON: Melissa, you are way too young for that old dance.

MELISSA: You aren't. Anyway, there's other things.

CLINTON: If I'd wanted to go, I'da gone.

MELISSA: There's the Pep Rally, maybe I wanted to be there? And all the kids in my class, they're hanging out outside the gym in the parking lot right now, and where am I? Clint, it's Friday night, it's Homecoming and I am at *home.* dammit!

CLINTON: Well you gotta admit, there is a kind of logic . . .

MELISSA: Don't make fun!

CLINTON: Hey – come on, sweet thing.

MELISSA: We were the only kids at the whole game who had to sit with their parents. Probably we were the only kids whose parents came. I was so embarrassed I wanted to die.

CLINTON: No you didn't.

(*Beat.*)

MELISSA: I'm not ever going to get grades like you.

CLINTON: Mellie. Give it time. You gotta work.

MELISSA: I don't want to be a representative of any damn thing!

CLINTON: I know, I know.

MELISSA: I represent me!

CLINTON: I know, honey. (*He holds her.*) And as such, you gotta get that grade-point up.

MELISSA: God, I hate you.

CLINTON: I know.

(*Trumpet rises, ceases, lights change.*)

◆ ◆ ◆ ◆

Clinton, 17; Julie, 17

In this scene, Clinton and his white girlfriend, Julie, sit outside the gym during a school Sadie Hawkins dance.

CLINTON: You cold? It's cold.

JULIE: I'm okay.

CLINTON: I mean, your thing, your dress, I was thinking you might be cold.

JULIE: You think it's too revealing?

CLINTON: No. No. I just thought you might be . . . My father did.

JULIE: What?

CLINTON: Thought your thing, your dress . . .

JULIE: God, really? How could you tell? He hardly said two words.

CLINTON: That's how I could tell.

JULIE: Well I'm sorry if I made a bad impression.

CLINTON: No. No. That's just him. I think you look fine. And this is . . . My Mom *did* dress me, can you believe it? (*Julie kisses him. Clinton responds, then pulls back.*) We just can't.

JULIE: Like my freckles?

CLINTON: Julie.

JULIE: They're eyebrow pencil. See?

CLINTON: Julie.

JULIE: They go all the way down.

CLINTON: Don't.

JULIE: I like you, Clinton, is that so very wrong?

CLINTON: You sound like a country-western song.
(*Beat.*)

JULIE: That wasn't very nice.

CLINTON: Please. I like you, too, Julie.

JULIE: Really?

CLINTON: Yes.

JULIE: It's funny. I believe you. When Tommy Sanders said stuff like that, I guess I just *wanted* to believe it. Why don't you have a driver's license?

CLINTON: I do. He just doesn't let me drive.

JULIE: You're kidding. That's kind of crazy.

CLINTON: Well you know. He needs his car. Vets get called out anytime, day or night.

JULIE: He doesn't *let* you?

CLINTON: I drive, I drive.

He wants me to succeed. "Kids in cars, they don't amount to a damn thing."

JULIE: At what?

CLINTON: What?

JULIE: Succeed at what?

CLINTON: Good question.

Being a Negro.

JULIE: God – really?

CLINTON: Oh, yeah, it's a riot, isn't it.

Right now half the kids in that gym are ready to kill me, maybe you didn't notice.

JULIE: I'm not stupid.

CLINTON: The jocks, the white ones, they're about to send out for rope. The black guys look at me and then they look at you in that . . . thing, and then they look at me again. And the black chicks? They won't bother with rope, they'll take me apart with their bare hands.

JULIE: At least they care about you.

CLINTON: What are. You talking. About.

JULIE: Your parents, they care.

CLINTON: Julie, you have an interesting mind.

JULIE: My mother, I'm lucky if she looks up when I walk in the room.

CLINTON: Maybe when you're changing the subject you could hold up one finger.

JULIE: I'm talking to you! I'm trying to talk to you.

CLINTON: Sorry.

JULIE: My mother, the biggest favor I could do for her is disappear. I know what the boys say about me, I know what Tommy

Sanders has been saying ever since Homecoming.

CLINTON: I don't hang out with those guys.

JULIE: But you know how they talk about me. 'Cause everybody says it. You know what they say. Don't you. Don't you.
(*Beat.*)

CLINTON: Yes.

JULIE: They say I'm easy. Well I'll tell you one thing, Clinton, easy is about the last thing it is.
(*Beat.*)

CLINTON: It ain't easy all over. Can I take you to Jake's?

JULIE: Now?

CLINTON: Cheeseburger deluxe and a double malt?

No Place To Be Somebody
By Charles Gordone

Cora, 20s; Shanty, 20s

No Place To Be Somebody, which was awarded a Pulitzer Prize in 1969 (the first to be awarded to an African-American playwright and the first Off-Broadway play to be so recognized), is a dynamic and compelling study of an ambitious black man named Johnny who owns a bar in a black neighborhood controlled by white thugs. When Johnny begins to buy property and attempts to get into the rackets himself, the local Mafia rough him up. Soon Johnny's life – including the lives of his closest friend and girlfriend – is irretrievably enmeshed in the machinations of the underworld, which leads to a violent conclusion.

In the scene below, Cora Beasley, a young black woman, and her boyfriend, Shanty Mulligan, a young white drummer, find themselves alone in Johnny's bar.

Shanty goes to door. Locks it. Punches up number on jukebox.

CORA: Shanty? I been doin' some thinkin'. You heard anything from Gloria?

SHANTY: Heard what?

CORA: 'Bout yo' divorce! Tha's what.

SHANTY: Gloria ain't gonna give me no die-vo'ce.

CORA: Well, if she ain't that don't stop us from livin' together, do it?

SHANTY: What made you change your mind?

CORA: 'Nother thing. Ever since I knowed you, you been bellyachin' 'bout gittin' you some drums.

SHANTY: Gonna git 'em too!

CORA: Well, I'm willin' to do everything I kin to help you.

SHANTY: You mean – you mean, you'd help me git 'em? No jive?

CORA: Then you could quit ol' Jay Cee an' go back to playin' in them nightclubs like you said you used to.

SHANTY: You really mean it? You'd help me git my drums?

CORA: Ain't talkin' jus' to hear myse'f rattle.

SHANTY: Mama, you are the greatest. (*He hugs her.*)

CORA: Honey, hush.

SHANTY: Know what I'm gonna do, Cora? Soon's I git them drums I'm gonna bring 'em in here. Set 'em up and play "the thing" for Johnny.

CORA: Lawd, Shanty! I wouldn't miss that for nothin' in this worl'.
(Shanty takes out a marijuana cigarette. Wets, lights it. Smokes.)
Lawd, Shanty! I done tole you 'bout smokin' them ol' nasty things.
(He passes the cigarette to her.)
(She grins.) Guess it won't hurt none once in a while.
(She inhales. Coughs.)

SHANTY: I was just thinkin' about ol' Gloria. How much she hated jazz. Nigger music, she called it. Man, every time I'd set up my skins to practice, she'd take the kids an' go over to her mother's.
(They begin to pass the cigarette back and forth.)
Dig? One night after a gig, brought some cats over for a little game. Some spade cat grabs her between the legs when I wasn't lookin'.

CORA: Spent the bes' part'a my life on Nigroes that won't no good. Had to baby an' take care of all of 'em.

SHANTY: Never heard the last of it. You'd think he raped her or somethin'.

CORA: Cain't hol' no job! Take yo' money and spen' it all on likker.

SHANTY: Got this job playin' the Borsch-Belt. My skins was shot! Had to borrow a set from Champ Jones.

CORA: Can't make up their min's. Jus' be a man, I says.

SHANTY: Gone about a week. Come home. Shades all down. Key won't fit in the door.

CORA: Git evil. Nex' thing you know they goin' up 'side yo' head.

SHANTY: She's over at her mother's. Says she gonna sue me for desershun.

CORA: I thought you was a dif'rent kind'a Nigger. I'm gon' git me a white man, one that'll take care me. Or he'p me take care myse'f.

SHANTY: I never did nothin' to her.

CORA: Tha's when he went up 'side my head with the ash tray!

SHANTY: Said she needed some bread. Went to the bank. Cashed my check. Come back. Skins the cat loaned me are gone.

CORA: I loved him so much.

SHANTY: Grabbed a broom out'a the closet. Went to work on the bitch.

CORA: Them awful things he said to me.

SHANTY: Bitch never made a soun' or dropped a tear.

CORA: I cried sump'm ter'ble.

SHANTY: Says I'd never see my kids ag'in or the drums neither.

CORA: Wanted children so bad! Doctor said I couldn't have none.

SHANTY: Started chokin' her. Would'a killed her, if my kid hadn't jumped on my back.

CORA: Ain't hard to satisfy me. 'Cause Lawd knows I ain't never asked for much.

SHANTY: One thing I learned. Stay away from bitches like that. Just ain't got no soul. (*He gets can of spray deodorant. Opens street doors and sprays the bar.*)

CORA: (*Rouses herself. Wipes tears.*) Shanty! I sho' wanna see Jay Cee's face when he sees you play them drums.
(*Blackout.*)

The Playboy Of The Western World
By John Millington Synge

Christy, 20s; Pegeen, 20s

In *The Playboy of the Western World* Christy Mahan, a shy Irish lad who is hired to clean pots in a small County Mayo pub, soon becomes the hero of the village when it is revealed that he has killed his tyrant of a father. Christy has the affections of a local widow—the publican's daughter, Pegeen Mike—and the other townspeople until old Mahan shows up wounded but very much alive. Despite these circumstances, Christy uses his new-found assurance to tame his father and then walks out on Pegeen Mike; he truly proves to be the "Playboy of the Western World."

In the scene that follows, Pegeen has just offered Christy a place to stay for the night.

PEGEEN: Let you stretch out now by the fire, young fellow. You should be destroyed travelling.

CHRISTY: (*Shyly again, drawing off his boots.*) I'm tired, surely, walking wild eleven days, and waking fearful in the night. (*He holds up one of his feet, feeling his blisters, and looking at them with compassion.*)

PEGEEN: (*Standing beside him, watching him with delight.*) You should have had great people in your family, I'm thinking, with the little, small feet you have, and you with a kind of a quality name, the like of what you'd find on the great powers and potentates of France and Spain.

CHRISTY: (*With pride.*) We were great surely, with wide and windy acres of rich Munster land.

PEGEEN: Wasn't I telling you, and you a fine, handsome young fellow with the noble brow?

CHRISTY: (*With a flash of delighted surprise.*) Is it me?

PEGEEN: Aye. Did you never hear that from the young girls where you come from in the west or south?

CHRISTY: (*With venom.*) I did not then. Oh, they're bloody liars in the naked parish where I grew a man.

PEGEEN: If they are itself, you've heard it these days, I'm thinking, and you walking the world telling out your story to young girls or old.

CHRISTY: I've told my story no place till this night, Pegeen Mike, and it's foolish I was here, maybe, to be talking free, but you're decent people, I'm thinking, and yourself a kindly woman, the way I wasn't fearing you at all.

PEGEEN: (*Filling a sack with straw.*) You've said the like of that, maybe, in every cot and cabin where you've met a young girl on your way.

CHRISTY: (*Going over to her, gradually raising his voice.*) I've said it nowhere till this night, I'm telling you, for I've seen none the like of you the eleven long days I am walking the world, looking over a low ditch or a high ditch on my north or my south, into stony scattered fields, or scribes of bog, where you'd see young, limber girls, and fine prancing women making laughter with the men.

PEGEEN: If you weren't destroyed travelling, you'd have as much talk and streeleen, I'm thinking, as Owen Roe O'Sullivan or the poets of Dingle Bay, and I've heard all times it's the poets are your like, fine fiery fellows with great rages when their temper's roused.

CHRISTY: (*Drawing a little nearer to her.*) You've a power of rings, God bless you, and would there be any offence if I was asking are you single now?

PEGEEN: What would I want wedding so young?

CHRISTY: (*With relief.*) We're alike, so.

PEGEEN: (*She puts sack on settle and beats it up.*) I never killed my father. I'd be afeard to do that, except I was the like of yourself with blind rages tearing me within, for I'm thinking you should have had great tussling when the end was come.

CHRISTY: (*Expanding with delight at the first confidential talk he has ever had with a woman.*) We had not then. It was a hard woman was come over the hill, and if he was always a crusty kind when he'd a hard woman setting on, not the divil himself or his four fathers could put up with him at all.

PEGEEN: (*With curiosity.*) And isn't it a great wonder that one wasn't fearing you?

CHRISTY: (*Very confidentially.*) Up to the day I killed my father, there wasn't a person in Ireland knew the kind I was, and I there drinking, waking, eating, sleeping, a quiet, simple poor fellow with no man giving me heed.

PEGEEN: (*Getting a quilt out of the cupboard and putting it on the sack.*) It was the girls were giving you heed maybe, and I'm thinking it's most conceit you'd have to be gaming with their like.

CHRISTY: (*Shaking his head, with simplicity.*) Not the girls itself, and I won't tell you a lie. There wasn't anyone heeding me in that place saving only the dumb beasts of the field.
(*He sits down at fire.*)

PEGEEN: (*With disappointment.*) And I thinking you should have been living the like of a king of Norway or the Eastern world.
(*She comes and sits beside him after placing bread and mug of milk on the table.*)

CHRISTY: (*Laughing piteously.*) The like of a king, is it? And I after toiling, moiling, digging, dodging from the dawn till dusk with never a sight of joy or sport saving only when I'd be abroad in the dark night poaching rabbits on hills, for I was a devil to poach, God forgive me, (*Very naïvely.*) and I near got six months for going with a dung fork and stabbing a fish.

PEGEEN: And it's that you'd call sport, is it, to be abroad in the darkness with yourself alone?

CHRISTY: I did, God help me, and there I'd be as happy as the sunshine of St. Martin's Day, watching the light passing the north or the patches of fog, till I'd hear a rabbit starting to screech and I'd go running in the furze. Then when I'd my full share I'd come walking down where you'd see the ducks and geese stretched sleeping on the highway of the road, and before I'd pass the dunghill, I'd hear himself snoring out, a loud lonesome snore he'd be making all times, the while he was sleeping, and he a man'd be raging all times, the while he was waking, like a gaudy officer you'd hear cursing and damning and swearing oaths.

PEGEEN: Providence and Mercy, spare us all!

CHRISTY: It's that you'd say surely if you seen him and he after drinking for weeks, rising up in the red dawn, or before it maybe, and going out into the yard as naked as an ash tree in the moon of May, and shying clods against the visage of the stars till he'd put the fear of death into the banbhs and the screeching sows.

PEGEEN: I'd be well-nigh afeard of that lad myself, I'm thinking. And there was no one in it but the two of you alone?

CHRISTY: The divil a one, though he'd sons and daughters walking all great states and territories of the world, and not a one of them, to this day, but would say their seven curses on him, and they rousing up to let a cough or sneeze, maybe, in the deadness of the night.

PEGEEN: (*Nodding her head.*) Well, you should have been a queer lot. I never cursed my father the like of that, though I'm twenty and more years of age.

CHRISTY: Then you'd have cursed mine, I'm telling you, and he a man never gave peace to any, saving when he'd get two months or three, or be locked in the asylums for battering peelers or assaulting men (*With depression.*) the way it was a bitter life he led me till I did up a Tuesday and halve his skull.

PEGEEN: (*Putting her hand on his shoulder.*) Well, you'll have peace in this place, Christy Mahon, and none to trouble you, and it's near time a fine lad like you should have your good share of the earth.

CHRISTY: It's time surely, and I a seemly fellow with great strength in me and bravery of . . .

(*Someone knocks.*)

(*Clinging to Pegeen.*) Oh, glory! It's late for knocking, and this last while I'm in terror of the peelers, and the walking dead.

Protest
By Norman Williams

Father, 40s; Daughter, 17

Canadian playwright Norman Williams' short play *Protest*, set in 1900, explores the unsettling change that occurs when traditional cultural values come into conflict with new ideas.

In the scene below, a young Japanese girl rebels against the customs of her ancestors by introducing a western chair into the home of her parents.

◆ ◆ ◆ ◆

FATHER: It's not a very comfortable chair, is it?

DAUGHTER: *We* aren't used to sitting in chairs.

FATHER: That is true. Still, I have done so before. (*The daughter shows interest.*) In the big cities they are quite commonly seen. But they aren't plain wooden ones like this. Some of them I have seen are made of shining brown cowhide; cool to the touch and so slippery I would be afraid to sit in one. Others are huge affairs with springs in the seat, and when you sit down it would seem you are sinking into a deep, soft cloud. I imagine the Westerners use them for sleeping. At least the ones I saw seated in them seemed on the verge of sleep.

DAUGHTER: Oh, there are so many things I have *never* seen.

FATHER: That is true of most of us, and many of the things we never see are right before our eyes all the time.

DAUGHTER: I didn't mean *those* things. I mean the new, wonderful things the Westerners have.

FATHER: (*Rises and takes the chair out, left.*) I will put this into the "shoe-off" room; it disturbs your grandmother.

DAUGHTER: And may I keep it in my room?

FATHER: We will have to think about that.

DAUGHTER: Ishimoto said it was a very fine chair and that houses in America had twenty or thirty each in them..

FATHER: (*Returns from left.*) So it was Ishimoto who gave you the chair? I guessed it was.

DAUGHTER: He didn't give it to me. I bought it.

FATHER: How could you buy it? You have no money. (*The father seats himself on one of the cushions, left.*)

DAUGHTER: I paid him with two of my pearl haircombs, my writing brush, and the red sash I had at New Year.

FATHER: And that is how Ishimoto grows richer day by day. Sit here opposite me, and let us talk together as we used to when you were a child. (*The daughter seats herself on the cushion opposite him.*) It is here, on this very spot, your old teacher used to teach you your lessons. Don't you remember any longer, with any fondness, all that he told you of our Japanese past, our culture and our wise men, our traditions, and the courageous lives of our history's heroines?

DAUGHTER: I only remember one thing about those lessons, my father.

FATHER: And what is that?

DAUGHTER: That all the two hours my old teacher sat where you sit now and droned into my ear our Japanese past, I was made to sit motionless, so. (*She assumes the rigid posture of the Japanese student.*) Never once was I allowed to move an arm, a hand, or my littlest finger. How the minutes dragged on! I thought he would never finish, that I would turn to stone on the spot and never be able to move again, or run and play in the courtyard.

FATHER: It is true the discipline was harsh –

DAUGHTER: One day, I remember, I felt my left foot grow numb and I ventured to move my trunk the tiniest fraction to relieve the pressure on it. My teacher saw me; he gave me a look like the black God of War. Without a word to me, he stopped the lesson; he got up and left without a bow. I could hear him in the next room complaining loudly to you and saying how unworthy I was. I was left crying with fear and shame.

FATHER: I remember.

DAUGHTER: From that day on, I had my lessons from him in the outer room with no heat, although it was December and the snow was piled high in the streets. I would turn purple with the cold, but dared not shiver or tremble in the slightest.

FATHER: Yes, yes. Your mother and I discussed it through an entire night.

DAUGHTER: I didn't know you noticed . . . or cared.

FATHER: We did. We were afraid it would be too hard on you but we decided, in the dawn light, rightly or wrongly, that discipline was the path to wisdom and virtue. We wanted our daughter to be wise and virtuous. We followed custom.

DAUGHTER: Custom!

FATHER: I know you think custom ancient and barbaric.

DAUGHTER: Yes, I do.

FATHER: Yet it is not. It does not diminish men's actions. It gives those actions form. It is our way of respecting others.

DAUGHTER: But it never changes. (*Proudly.*) This is the year 1900, you know.

FATHER: (*Amused.*) A Western year. 1900, eh? Did Mr. Ishimoto give you that information? Perhaps free, with the chair?

DAUGHTER: (*With child-like mysteriousness.*) Oh, I had heard what year it was.

FATHER: Will you believe me If I tell you something?

DAUGHTER: I will try.

FATHER: It is not true that custom fails to change.

DAUGHTER: I don't see that it does.

FATHER: You have not observed it long enough. Do you know there was a day when meat was never eaten in this house? To eat meat was looked upon as a loathsome evil because the Buddha himself forbade the killing of animals. But gradually the belief began to change. Little by little we were invaded by new ideas from the Western world. I well remember the day I first ordered the preparation of meat in this house. My honoured mother spent that day in her room at her personal shrine praying for all of us who dared to break a tradition over a thousand years old. She ate nothing for three days and for two years and more would not eat with us in this room or go near the kitchen where the meat was prepared. To this very

hour she has never tasted it and will not if she lives another
hundred years.

DAUGHTER: She is stubborn.

FATHER: We must all be stubborn in what we believe or one day
find we believe in nothing.

DAUGHTER: But you said you change your beliefs.

FATHER: I do, and have, and will. When others began to eat meat, I
said to myself: Is there some good in this? And I inquired and
found there was; that animal flesh makes men stronger and
builds muscles to withstand cold and hard work. And so I said,
"I will change. We will eat meat in my house." And we did.
But not until I had considered it carefully and weighed the
custom against the new belief.

DAUGHTER: Perhaps you have changed – in small things.

FATHER: Small things?

DAUGHTER: Eating meat is a small thing to me when I see how
chained our lives are.

FATHER: We are not chained. We are civilized and reserved, it is
true –

DAUGHTER: You call it civilized and reserved, but I call it a prison. I
am in a prison and I yearn to be free.

(*Enter mother at centre back. She carries a bowl, crosses to
the table and places the bowl on it. She putters about as an
excuse for eavesdropping.*)

FATHER: Free to do as you please?

DAUGHTER: Free to do as –

FATHER: As – what?

DAUGHTER: As other women do.

FATHER: What other women?

DAUGHTER: Western women.

FATHER: Ishimoto!

DAUGHTER: Mr. Ishimoto has told me many things; he has painted
me a picture of another world – a world I long to know and
be a part of. In that world, women are free to grow and
blossom instead of sitting with folded hands and allowing life
to slip away from them as they do here.

FATHER: Women here live honourable lives.

DAUGHTER: (*Flatly.*) They obey their husbands and bear children and die with never a question on their lips.

FATHER: Is that not honourable?

DAUGHTER: It is not freedom. In the Western lands women do not hide behind shutters and sit in an eternal twilight while others regulate their lives.

FATHER: They do not?

DAUGHTER: No. There they walk freely on the streets or go into tea-houses alone and order what they wish and pay for it themselves, for they have their own money.

FATHER: I have heard of that.

DAUGHTER: But, most important, they go to school and learn what men learn. They talk to men as their equals and, Mr. Ishimoto says, a wife may even criticize her husband.
(*The mother, who has listened in growing horror, utters an exclamation at this and hurriedly leaves the room.*)

FATHER: My daughter –

DAUGHTER: And it is said that men embrace their wives in front of others and show affection in ways I don't properly understand. But I know it is by more than a bow.

FATHER: It is. I have heard of it. It is called kissing.

DAUGHTER: That's it. That is what Mr. Ishimoto called it.

FATHER: But a kiss is only another custom, strange to us but familiar to them. There is as much feeling of the heart in a bow as there is in a kiss. And yet, to my mind, a bow is in good form because it is an unselfish recognition of another; while a kiss, which is part of love-making, shows a desire for one's own pleasure.

DAUGHTER: It sounds exciting and natural to me.

FATHER: What is natural and what is not? It would seem that all of life must be regulated in some way if we are to live together. One could argue that it is "natural" to have customs to regulate "naturalness."

DAUGHTER: (*Boldly, then hesitatingly.*) I think it is natural for –

FATHER: For what?

DAUGHTER: For a girl to choose her own husband.

FATHER: (*Rises.*) What do you say? Oh, this is too much. I have sat here patiently trying to reason with you, but this is too much.

DAUGHTER: I don't want to marry a man I've never seen.

FATHER: Ungrateful, unfilial child! What do you know, what does any young girl know about choosing a husband? What can she know of his means, his family, his character, his education, which are what matter in a husband?

DAUGHTER: I *won't!* I *won't* marry him.

FATHER: I draw the line. Finally and firmly. Have all the romantic daydreams you like – no doubt your husband will pay for them – but you *will* marry the man we have chosen for you.

DAUGHTER: (*Beating her hands on the floor.*) No, no, no, no.

FATHER: This is my fault. I should have supervised your education.

DAUGHTER: (*Sobbing.*) Education.

FATHER: But the education of a daughter is always in the hands of the women of the house.

DAUGHTER: (*Triumphantly.*) There, you see? Another *custom!*

A Raisin In The Sun
By Lorraine Hansberry

Asagai, 20s; Beneatha, 18-20

Set in a Chicago ghetto in the 1950s, *A Raisin in the Sun* is the story of how three generations of an African-American family, the Youngers, overcome their conflicts and bring their divergent hopes and dreams into common focus.

In the scene that follows, Beneatha, who has just learned the disturbing news that her sister Ruth is pregnant, welcomes Asagai, a student from Nigeria, into her home.

ASAGAI: Hello, Alaiyo –

BENEATHA: (*Holding the door open and regarding him with pleasure.*) Hello . . . (*Long pause.*) Well – come in. And please excuse everything. My mother was very upset about my letting anyone come here with the place like this.

ASAGAI: (*Coming into the room.*) You look disturbed too . . . Is something wrong?

BENEATHA: (*Still at the door, absently*) Yes . . . we all got acute ghetto-itus. (*She smiles and comes toward him, finding a cigarette and sitting.*) So – sit down! How was Canada?

ASAGAI: (*A sophisticate.*) Canadian.

BENEATHA: (*Looking at him.*) I'm very glad you are back.

ASAGAI: (*Looking back at her in turn.*) Are you really?

BENEATHA: Yes – very.

ASAGAI: Why – you were quite glad when I went away. What happened?

BENEATHA: You went away.

ASAGAI: Ahhhhhhhh.

BENEATHA: Before – you wanted to be so serious before there was time.

ASAGAI: How much time must there be before one knows what one feels?

BENEATHA: (*Stalling this particular conversation. Her hands pressed*

together, in a deliberately childish gesture.) What did you
bring me?

ASAGAI: (*Handing her the package.*) Open it and see.

BENEATHA: (*Eagerly opening the package and drawing out some
records and the colorful robes of a Nigerian woman.*) Oh,
Asagai! . . . You got them for me! . . . How beautiful . . . and
the records too! (*She lifts out the robes and runs to the mirror
with them and holds the drapery up in front of herself.*)

ASAGAI: (*Coming to her at the mirror.*) I shall have to teach you
how to drape it properly. (*He flings the material about her for
the moment and stands back to look at her.*) Ah – *Oh-pay-
gay-day, oh-gbah-mu-shay.* [*A Yoruba exclamation for
admiration.*] You wear it well . . . very well . . . mutilated hair
and all.

BENEATHA: (*Turning suddenly.*) My hair – what's wrong with my
hair?

ASAGAI: (*Shrugging.*) Were you born with it like that?

BENEATHA: (*Reaching up to touch it.*) No . . . of course not. (*She
looks back into the mirror, disturbed.*)

ASAGAI: (*Smiling.*) How then?

BENEATHA: You know perfectly well how . . . as crinkly as yours . . .
that's how.

ASAGAI: And it is ugly to you that way?

BENEATHA: (*Quickly.*) Oh, no – not ugly . . . (*More slowly,
apologetically.*) but it's hard to manage when it's, well – raw.

ASAGAI: And so to accommodate that – you mutilate it every week?

BENEATHA: It's not mutilation!

ASAGAI: (*Laughing aloud at her seriousness.*) Oh . . . please! I am
only teasing you because you are so very serious about these
things. (*He stands back from her and folds his arms across his
chest as he watches her pulling at her hair and frowning in the
mirror.*) Do you remember the first time you met me at
school? . . . (*He laughs.*) You came up to me and you said –
and I thought you were the most serious little thing I had ever
seen – you said: (*He imitates her.*) "Mr. Asagai – I want very
much to talk with you. About Africa. You see, Mr. Asagai, I'm

looking for my *identity!*" (*He laughs.*)

BENEATHA: (*Turning to him, not laughing.*) Yes – (*Her face is quizzical, profoundly disturbed.*)

ASAGAI: (*Still teasing and reaching out and taking her face in his hands and turning her profile to him.*) Well . . . it is true that this is not so much a profile of a Hollywood queen as perhaps a queen of the Nile – (*A mock dismissal of the importance of the question.*) – but what does it matter? Assimilationism is so popular in your country.

BENEATHA: (*Wheeling, passionately, sharply.*) I am not an assimilationist!

ASAGAI: (*The protest hangs in the room for a moment and Asagai studies her, his laughter fading.*) Such a serious one. (*There is a pause.*) So – you like the robes? You must take excellent care of them – they are from my sister's personal wardrobe.

BENEATHA: (*With incredulity.*) You – you sent all the way home – for me?

ASAGAI: (*With charm.*) For you – I would do much more . . . Well, that is what I came for. I must go.

BENEATHA: Will you call me Monday?

ASAGAI: Yes . . . we have a great deal to talk about. I mean about identity and time and all that.

BENEATHA: Time?

ASAGAI: Yes. About how much time one needs to know what one feels.

BENEATHA: You never understood that there is more than one kind of feeling which can exist between a man and a woman – or, at least, there should be.

ASAGAI: (*Shaking his head negatively but gently.*) No. Between a man and a woman there need be only one kind of feeling. I have that for you . . . now even . . . right this moment . . .

BENEATHA: I know – and by itself – it won't do. I can find that anywhere.

ASAGAI: For a woman it should be enough.

BENEATHA: I know – because that's what it says in all the novels that men write. But it isn't. Go ahead and laugh – but I'm not

interested in being someone's little episode in America or –
(*With feminine vengeance.*) – one of them! (*Asagai has burst
into laughter again.*) That's funny as hell, huh!

ASAGAI: it's just that every American girl I have known has said that
to me. White – black – in this you are all the same. And the
same speech, too!

BENEATHA: (*Angrily.*) Yuk, yuk, yuk!

ASAGAI: It's how you can be sure that the world's most liberated
women are not liberated at all. You all talk about it too much!

Rancho Hollywood
By Carlos Morton

Jed, late 20s; Ramona, teens

Rancho Hollywood is a farcical and exaggerated look at the history of California from just before the Gold Rush of 1849 to the present. Exposing the "false images" of Latino, Black, and Native Americans that Hollywood has perpetuated, the play loosely follows historical facts as it parodies Hollywood's vision and shatters the myth; real names of many of the characters have been changed to underscore the theme, e.g., Jedediah Smith becomes Jedediah Goldbanger Smith, Pío Pico becomes Río Pico.

In the scene below, Jedediah Goldbanger Smith, a Yankee trader-trapper-goldminer-soldier-capitalist with a vision, covets Ramona Rico, the young daughter of California's last Mexican Governor.

JED: (*Out on his balcony, next to Ramona's balcony. Looking at her covetously.*) Buenas tardes, Señorita Ramona.

RAMONA: Buenas tardes, Mister Smith.

JED: Looks like it's going to be a beautiful sunset there on the sea. (*She nods but does not answer.*) What do you call those mountains to the north?

RAMONA: Las Moñtanas de San Bernardino.

JED: And the valley?

RAMONA: El Valle de San Fernando.

JED: A little too much smog today.

RAMONA: Smog? What's that?

JED: Smog is what you get when General Motors, Firestone, and the Oil Companies buy up the Electric Trolley Car system.

RAMONA: Oh. (*Not wishing to appear ignorant of the latest inventions.*) We are very isolated from the rest of the world here in California. We have no electric trolley car systems like you do back East. We do have El Mar del Pacifico.

JED: Oh yes, there's Marine Land. Say, which way are the pyramids from here?

RAMONA: Oh, Señor, we have no pyramids here in La Cuidad de La

Reina de Los Angeles del Rio Porciúncula.

JED: Is that the full name of this city? Isn't it rather long? Why don't you just call it Los Angeles, or L.A.?

RAMONA: El Lay? Sounds obscene! But Los Angeles, the city of the Angels, sounds heavenly.

JED: My God! I've suddenly been struck with a vision!

RAMONA: What, what's the matter?

JED: The city, it's burning! It's the city of Lost Angels. We're in Hell!

RAMONA: I see nothing; no smoke, fire, hell.

JED: Look, the freeways! The Pomona, San Diego, Santa Monica, Santa Ana! Millions of automobiles snaking along, exhaust fumes trailing. There, the Harbor Freeway, Golden State, Long Beach! Endless miles of concrete!

RAMONA: Señor, where do you see this?

JED: My God! It's enough to curdle your blood. Look there, tall buildings, scraping the skies! Airports; with planes stacked up like saucers in holding patterns! Marinas glutting the shoreline! Stadiums, with millions of sports fans growling in unison! And slums, slums everywhere! East L.A.! Watts! It's burning, it's burning!

RAMONA: Señor, Señor, what can I do?

JED: My mind is burning! Give me some water!

RAMONA: (*Dousing Jed with a flowerpot.*) Are you all right?

JED: Yes, yes, just a momentary burst of apocalyptic prophecy. I'm all right. I have fits, er, visions. I'll be OK.

RAMONA: Do you see any vision or future for yourself here in our city?

JED: Yes, I'd like a little piece of land. Say, Orange County. I'll develop, but modestly, in harmony with the environment. A few condos, 7-11's.

RAMONA: We have a very liberal immigration policy, there being but 6,000 of us and so much land for the taking. My father is the Governor, he could give you a land grant.

JED: Your father, does he like Yankees?

RAMONA: Only Mexicanized Yankees. We have quite a few, you know, who have come here and adapted our ways, intermarried with our people.

JED: Tell me, your father, how does he feel about an independent California?

RAMONA: Don't let him hear you say that! He's a staunch Mexican all the way. But I know that we must leave the Fatherland some day.

JED: There you go! Join our Union! Go the American way!

RAMONA: What can you offer us Californios?

JED: Protection from foreign encroachment, for one thing. Those Russians are sneaky, just look how fast they got into Cuba. Besides security, I can give you undreamt of wealth, and a future with a vision never before seen on earth. I can give you apple pie and motorboat races, hamburgers and Disneyland! (*Kneeling.*) Marry me!

RAMONA: Señor, please, this sort of thing is not done here in Rancho Madera Acebo. There are proper channels, traditions. Besides, I will not marry outside my race, my class.

JED: Rancho Mad Era Azebo. What does that translate to?

RAMONA: Literally, it means Rancho of the Wood Holly.

JED: Hollywood! Hollywood! Hollywood and Vine. Groman's Chinese Theatre, the Brown Derby. The Film Industry! Television!

RAMONA: Are you having a fit again? Look at your eyes, they are like shooting stars.

JED: I'll open a string of porno shops. I'll do snuff films. Life is cheap in Latin America. No, just kidding. (*Pulls out photograph.*) Look, see this photograph of my mother, let me explain. See, someday, we'll be able to run thousands of these together into moving pictures which will be projected on a screen and be able to reach an audience of millions. Well, here, I'll make you a camera. (*Jed fashions a little box, climbs over into her balcony.*)

RAMONA: Un momento, por favor. Slow down. This is your mother? What's her name? Where is she from?

JED: Her name is Goldie. This was taken in Europe. She's dead now, of a broken heart, but that's another story. I am her son, her only son. Promised I would carry her picture with me forever.

RAMONA: Are you Anglo-Saxon?

JED: Yes, yes, of course, isn't everyone? Except for you, who are Spanish.

RAMONA: Yes, of course. But with a dash of Indian, for spice.

JED: Your father, he is very dark.

RAMONA: He goes outdoors a lot, a sun worshipper. Your mother, she looks very exotic, her clothes, her features, almost Oriental.

JED: She's part Polish.

RAMONA: I see.

JED: Well, Señorita Ramona Rico, I guess I better go and get some shut eye. I got a long day of colonizing ahead of me tomorrow. But first, how about a good night kiss? In our country it's perfectly proper to kiss a girl on the first date. Some couples go even further. Have you heard of Women's Liberation?

RAMONA: No! (*As he tries to put his arms around her.*) No!

JED: Well then, how about a stage kiss, it's only make believe?

RAMONA: (*Pushing him over the balcony.*) Mañana! (*She exits.*)

JED: No, never say mañana! It's today. Eureka, I've found it! Hollywood, Hollywood!
(*Blackout.*)

The Slab Boys
By John Byrne

Lucille, 19-22; Phil, 19

"The Slab Boys" of John Byrne's title are three young men who work mixing and matching paints for a carpet company in Scotland. Each of the boys dreams of a better life, perhaps a future that would elevate his place in the world beyond that of his parents. Phil dreams of going to art school but is constantly worried that the mental illness that has tormented his mother for years is somehow in his future as well.

In the first scene, Phil attempts to get a date with Lucille ("every slab boy's dream").

◆ ◆ ◆ ◆

LUCILLE: What've youse been saying to Jack Hogg? He's sitting out there with his face like a half-chewed Penny Dainty.

PHIL: Aw, it's clearing up, is it?

LUCILLE: Bernadette Rooney's boyfriend's going to come up here and give you and your pal a doing if you don't hang off.

PHIL: Hang off what?

LUCILLE: Jack Hogg. They went to school together.

PHIL: Tremble . . . tremble . . .

LUCILLE: It's only Bernadette that's holding him back from coming.

PHIL: Ah, she's a Catholic?

LUCILLE: Eh?

PHIL: Nothing. (*Pause.*) Er . . . tell me something, Lucille . . .

LUCILLE: God, is there never any dishes washed in this Slab?

PHIL: See the new guy?

LUCILLE: What new guy? Aw . . . him . . . yeh, what about him?

PHIL: Nothing, nothing . . . Just wondered what you thought about him, that's all.

LUCILLE: He's allright. How?

PHIL: Just asking . . .

LUCILLE: What've you asking for?

PHIL: You know he's got scruffula, don't you?

LUCILLE: He's got what?

PHIL: Scruffula. Like very bad impetigo . . . only worse.

LUCILLE: Who told you that rubbish?

PHIL: He caught it off Jack. Tough eh?

LUCILLE: Quit acting it, you.

PHIL: I'm serious. Of course, it's dormant at the moment but any minute his face could just erupt. Him and Jack's been pally for years . . . Used to live next door to each other . . .

LUCILLE: I never knew that . . .

PHIL: I mean, Jack's as upset about it as everybody else . . . Arthur included . . .

LUCILLE: I thought his name was Alan?

PHIL: Arthur . . . Alan . . . makes no odds. Another couple of weeks and nobody's going to recognise anyhow. Face'll be eaten away totally . . . Just like Jacky Boy's.

LUCILLE: I thought what Jack had wasn't infectious. He told Miss Walkinshaw he's getting treatment for it . . .

PHIL: He would say that, sweetheart. He's what you call a 'carrier', you see. Like some people are carriers for infantile paralysis . . . some are carriers for smallpox . . . Jack's a carrier for plooks. 'Course, you're okay if you've got 'natural immunity' like I've got . . . look at that . . . clear as a baby's. (*Shoves his face up next to Lucille.*)

LUCILLE: Gerroff!

PHIL: Not young Aldo, I'm afraid . . . D'you ever see that movie where the guy gets buried up to his chin in quicksands and they put this cardboard box full of soldier ants over his noggin and pour treacle through a pin-hole in the top?

LUCILLE: Stop that, you!

PHIL: That's how his features'll be in about three weeks. There's no known cure for it . . .

LUCILLE: Give us that dish. (*Snatches dish and crosses to sink. Starts washing it.*)

PHIL: Er . . . Lucille . . .

LUCILLE: What?

PHIL: I was . . . er wondering . . .

LUCILLE: Wondering what? Don't start on about folk with half-eaten-away faces, I'm warning you.

PHIL: No . . . I was wondering if you'd er . . .

LUCILLE: Wondering if I'd what?

PHIL: If you'd like to . . . er . . .

(*Just then a face appears at the dirty window. It is Hector half visible through the dirty glass. He has a bloodstained rag knotted 'round his head. He is in his underwear.*)

LUCILLE: Like to what?

PHIL: (*In a rush.*) If you'd like to go to the Staffie with me?

LUCILLE: (*Sees face at window.*) Aaaaaaaaaaaaaaaaaaaargh! (*Exits.*)

Lucille, 19-22; Spanky, 19

In this scene, Phil's chum, Spanky, tries to get the same girl to go to the same dance.

SPANKY: Hi Lucille. Replenishing the old 'jooga di aqua', I see.

LUCILLE: You trying to be filthy again?

SPANKY: It's Italian . . .

LUCILLE: Where'd you get it . . . off a chip poke?

SPANKY: D'you hear about Hector?

LUCILLE: Hear what?

SPANKY: He's going to be leaving us . . .

LUCILLE: Am I supposed to pass out or something? You should all be leaving. You're a bunch of good-for-nothing foul-mouthed pigs . . . in a foul-smelling pig sty. Take a look at this joint . . . what d'you see?

SPANKY: We're waiting for the decorators . . .

LUCILLE: It's an absolute cowp. You're frightened to come in here in case you get something contagious. And by the way that isn't true what you said about the new guy . . . I checked with Jack. What Jack's got is described as 'Parched Skin' . . . and it is not smittal, so there.

SPANKY: Ah . . . that's good news.

LUCILLE: You're a bunch of lying dogs. And you're bone idle . . .

look at all them manky dishes.

SPANKY: Let lying dogs sleep, I always say. Er . . . Lucille, I was wondering . . .

LUCILLE: Here we go again. Yes?

SPANKY: I was wondering if you . . . er . . . caught my drift earlier on?

LUCILLE: And what drift was that?

SPANKY: The Staffie . . . ?

LUCILLE: The Staffie?

SPANKY: Staff Dance . . .

LUCILLE: Aw . . . that's what you call it? How childish.

SPANKY: If you fancied going with . . . ?

LUCILLE: Fancied going with who? Not you?

SPANKY: Yeah . . . what's up with me? I know you aren't booked . . .

LUCILLE: Oh, do you?

SPANKY: I checked with Miss Walkinshaw. How about it, eh? I'm getting a gadgey suit from "Caled . . . " from "Jackson's" . . . real honey . . . roll collar . . . swivel button . . . fingertip drape . . . Yeh, I know my arms look a bit on the long side but the guy in the shop said that was no problem . . . he's going to break them off at the elbows for us. What d'you say? Eh? What're you staring at?

LUCILLE: I can't believe the cheek of you guys. Have you looked in a mirror lately?

SPANKY: 'Course I have . . . every morning when I'm shaving. I've got a very heavy growth, you know. Feel.

LUCILLE: Don't come near me.

SPANKY: C'mon, cut the capers, Lucille . . . are you going to the Dance or are you not going to the Dance?

LUCILLE: Oh, I'm going okay . . .

SPANKY: Terrific. What time d'you want me to . . . ?

LUCILLE: But not with you, sonny boy. I'm booked.

SPANKY: What? Who're you going with? I never heard nothing.

LUCILLE: That's because your listeners are run up from the same material as your rompers . . . shoddy flannelette.

SPANKY: C'mon, who is it? Who are you going with?

LUCILLE: Excuse me . . .

SPANKY: Don't be lousy . . . tell me who it is.

LUCILLE: All I'm saying is . . .

SPANKY: Yeh?

LUCILLE: . . . It's someone from the Slab Room. Now, shift.

SPANKY: Eh?

LUCILLE: Shift, I said. Move the torso.

SPANKY: Sure . . .

    (*Enter Phil.*)

PHIL: Ah . . . Lucille . . . help yourself to a cork-tipped Woodbine . . . Don't scar the chest, throat or lungs . . . just tear the skin off your lips. On you go, I've got hundreds . . .

Take A Giant Step
By Louis Peterson

Christine, late 20s; Spence, 17

Take A Giant Step depicts the coming of age of Spence, a young African-American boy who experiences a sense of estrangement from his white friends as he emerges into adulthood. Confused by the prejudices of the adult world, his anger leads to his expulsion from school and a series of low life encounters that leave him even more bewildered. It is not until he has a confrontation with his parents, confides his fears in the family maid, and experiences the death of his grandmother that he is able to make sense of what he may become.

In Act Two, Scene 2, Spence, who has been recovering from illness and the death of his grandmother, encounters a young woman who is set on taking care of him.

CHRISTINE: You know, I've met many a mulish critter in my day, but you're the worst mule I've ever met. Now you ain't asleep because I heard you tipping around up here not ten minutes ago. Now open your eyes and eat your lunch.

SPENCE: I don't want it.

CHRISTINE: (*Crosses with tray to bureau.*) You know you don't have to eat it? You know that, don't you? But don't blame anyone but yourself when your bones are rattling around inside your skin like two castanets hit together – you understand? I suppose you don't want your medicine either. (*Crosses Up of bed.*) Boy, you sure do beat all. You're the stubbornest cuss I ever met. I'll ask you one more time. Are you going to take this medicine or aren't you? Speak up, 'cause I don't have all day.

SPENCE: No.

CHRISTINE: I didn't quite catch that. Don't be mumbling at me, boy. Was it "Yes" or "No" that you said?

SPENCE: I said "No."

CHRISTINE: Boy, you know you're going to make some girl a pretty miserable husband one of these days. Course, you know, I don't believe you're not eating. (*Crosses to bureau.*) I think you sneak downstairs after I leave and eat everything in sight. (*Pause.*) Did you hear me?

(*No answer.*)

(*Crosses to bed.*) Spence, won't you please sit up and eat something? Anything? Crust of bread? You know it kills me when folks don't eat.

(*No answer.*) I never knew anybody who could pick out just the right way to worry somebody. Won't you eat just a little bit?

SPENCE: (*Head up in bed.*) I said "No."

CHRISTINE: (*Crosses to chair for pillow slip, returns.*) Well, I guess that settles it – don't it? Then you can get out of bed so I can make it.

SPENCE: You don't need to make it today.

CHRISTINE: The devil you say. I've taken enough from you today already. Now just get out of that bed before I pick you up and throw you out of it. You're not supposed to stay in bed all day anyway. The doctor said to get up and walk around and to get some air if you felt like it.

SPENCE: Don't you get sick of repeating yourself?

CHRISTINE: (*Crosses to bureau, returns with decanter.*) You've got till I count three. One – two – three – (*Throws water.*)

SPENCE: (*Throwing the covers off and laughing in spite of himself.*) All right – all right. I'm getting up now. (*He goes Right and sits in chair.*) You make me sick.

CHRISTINE: The feeling is oh so mutual. (*She begins to make the bed – stands above it.*) I've seen a mess of mourning in my day, but if the mourning you do don't beat anything I've ever seen yet, I don't want a nickel. But at the rate you're going you're not going to have much longer to mourn. You're going to be joining them that you're mournin' for if you don't watch your step.

SPENCE: What do you say to my making a little bargain with you?

CHRISTINE: What is it?

SPENCE: I'll eat that slop that you brought up here if as soon as that bed is made you get the hell out of here and leave me alone.

CHRISTINE: (*Takes food tray from chair to bureau.*) There ain't no call to be rude and nasty. All I'm saying is that you look like a bag of bones and you do.

SPENCE: I've always been skinny.

CHRISTINE: (*Pours medicine in soup.*) It's humanly impossible for somebody to be as skinny as you are and live. Consumption is chasing you in one direction and pneumonia is chasing you in the other – and when they meet with you in the middle, it's sure enough going to be a mess.

SPENCE: Why don't you shut up?

CHRISTINE: (*Moves to above bed, continues making it.*) Why don't you eat your lunch instead of sitting up there looking like death warmed over?

SPENCE: (*Gets out of the chair and viciously picks up the tray from the bureau; brings it back, sits down with it and begins to eat.*) Now will you let me alone?

CHRISTINE: (*Crosses to bureau, gets out socks.*) Who's bothering you?

SPENCE: You are.

CHRISTINE: (*Crosses to him, puts wrapper around shoulders.*) Aw! Go on, boy. You know you love it.

SPENCE: (*Tasting the soup.*) What kind of soup is this?

CHRISTINE: (*Putting on left sock.*) What'd you say?

SPENCE: I said, "What kind of soup is this?"

CHRISTINE: Chicken.

SPENCE: Well, it tastes damn peculiar. (*Tasting it again.*) What's in it?

CHRISTINE: Nothing.

SPENCE: What's in this soup? (*Pause.*) You put the medicine in this soup.

CHRISTINE: Does it taste awful?

SPENCE: It tastes like hell. You sure are a lousy cook. No wonder you can't keep a husband.

CHRISTINE: I'll have you know that I've only had one husband – and he died.

SPENCE: I'm not surprised.

CHRISTINE: (*Throws socks down, rises, crosses to bed, works on sheets.*) I'm not speaking to you again today. And that's final.

SPENCE: You're not really mad are you, Christine? (*Pause.*) Christine, I was just kidding. (*Pause.*) Aw! Come on, Christine. You know I don't really think that you killed your husband.

CHRISTINE: (*Laughing. Crosses to Spence.*) Boy you sure are a mess. (*They look at one another.*) You feel better now – don't you?

SPENCE: I guess so.

CHRISTINE: (*Puts on right sock.*) You're getting some color in your cheeks.

SPENCE: Don't you think you're hurrying things a little, Christine? I haven't finished eating yet.

CHRISTINE: If there's one thing I can't stand it's skinny men around me. Never could stand skinny men since I can first remember. You wouldn't be a bad-looking boy if you just weren't so skinny.

SPENCE: Thanks, Christine. Thanks. You're a real tin pitcher full of complaints today. You're as generous with the old complaints as Gram. (*He stops eating.*)

CHRISTINE: (*Rises, stands over Spence Left of him.*) Now what's the matter? What've you stopped eating for?

SPENCE: You know what's the matter.

CHRISTINE: (*Fixes something on tray.*) Now there isn't any point in thinking about that now.

SPENCE: I know there isn't, but I can't help it.

CHRISTINE: Just don't think about it.

SPENCE: That's a very stupid thing to say. You can't just stop thinking about someone because they're dead, can you?

CHRISTINE: Yes, yes you can if you want to. You just don't open the door and let yourself in, that's all.

SPENCE: What are you talking about?

CHRISTINE: Nothing. Now eat your lunch. (*To Above bed.*)

SPENCE: (*Begins eating again.*) You know, it's funny. I got expelled from school – Gram died – and I got sick – and so I couldn't go to school anyway – even if they hadn't kicked me out.

Funny the way things turn out.

CHRISTINE: Yes, it is – isn't it? (*She stops work, listens.*)

SPENCE: You know, Christine, I was just thinking. 'Course last week was the funeral and I figure maybe the guys didn't want to come and see me then. But I've been home all this week. (*Christine crosses to him, gets tray.*)
Wouldn't you have thought that one of them would have come over to see me by now?

CHRISTINE: (*Putting tray on bureau.*) Nothing surprises me any more.

SPENCE: What do you mean by that?

CHRISTINE: Nothing. (*Feels his head.*) I don't think you have any more fever. You want to take your temperature?

SPENCE: Naw! (*Pause.*) Your hands are very warm, Christine.

CHRISTINE: Warm hands – warm heart.

SPENCE: That would be fine except that that's not the way it goes.

CHRISTINE: (*Crossing to bed.*) It goes that way for me, and that's what matters.

SPENCE: (*Rises, crosses to Right of Bureau.*) Were you born here, Christine?

CHRISTINE: No. I was born in Alabama. Birmingham, Alabama, in Ensley, near the steel mills.

SPENCE: I'll bet you didn't like it much down there, did you?

CHRISTINE: No, I didn't like it much down there.

SPENCE: Is your family still there?

CHRISTINE: (*Crosses Down in front of bed. Changes pillow slip.*) My father was killed in the mills when I was a little girl. My ma died a couple of years ago. I had two brothers and two sisters. I don't know where they are now.

SPENCE: (*Crosses to bed, sits.*) What made you come way the hell up here by yourself?

CHRISTINE: (*Laughing.*) I wanted something better, I guess. I decided I was coming up North to try my luck. I worked for a whole year before I'd saved the money, and the day I had what I thought was enough, I went down to the railroad station. (*Stops work.*) Boy, that was some day! The sun was shining and I felt real good like you feel maybe once or twice in your whole life. When I got to the ticket window, the man had a calendar, and it had an advertisement for a big insurance company on it. So I looked at the name of the town and then I told him that that's where I wanted my ticket to take me. Then I went home and packed my mama's cardboard suitcase, and that same night I caught the train. And that's the last I ever saw of my mother and my brothers and sisters and Rusty.

SPENCE: Who the hell was Rusty?

CHRISTINE: (*Sits at head of bed. Spence sits in the middle.*) Rusty was my dog. Well, I didn't go to work for the insurance company. I went into service for a while and then I got married. And that's what I meant when I was telling you about the doors. See, my husband died about two years after that and about two months after he died, I had a baby and he was born dead.

SPENCE: Christine!

CHRISTINE: Well, I tell you for a while I felt like all I wanted to do was die myself. Then I realized that you just can't go on like that. It's like your mind is divided into little rooms and each time you go back into one of those little rooms your heart likes to break in two. So all you do is shut the doors – and lock them – to those little rooms in your mind and never let yourself in them again. So I've got two little locked rooms in my mind. One for Bert, my husband, and one for my baby that never had a name. Do you want some more to eat?

SPENCE: No, Christine, I don't think so. You sure do make me feel crummy, Christine.

CHRISTINE: Why?

SPENCE: Well, I've been giving you a pretty hard time about what's been happening to me. (*Pause.*) I'm sorry, Christine.

CHRISTINE: That's all right, boy. You're just unhappy – that's all. But you'll get used to that. Pretty soon you'll be able to laugh a little bit and make jokes, even while you're unhappy. It won't be this bad forever. (*Rises.*) Well, the bed's made, the house is clean, and you've had your lunch. So –

SPENCE: Don't go, Christine. Stay with me.

CHRISTINE: (*Crossing to bureau for tray.*) I've got another cleaning job, boy.

SPENCE: Just for a little while longer. (*Pause.*) If you have to go, well then I guess you have to, but if you could stay just a little while longer it would mean a lot to me. It isn't that I'm afraid of anything, but I get to thinking about all the things I've got to do.

CHRISTINE: What have you got to do?

SPENCE: Well, I've got to really get well – first of all. I'll take the medicine and I'll take a hell of a lot of vitamins and I figure that'll fix me up all right.

CHRISTINE: (*Crossing to him with pills.*) There's no time like the present to begin.

SPENCE: Honest, Christine.

CHRISTINE: A little water? (*She gets water glass from tray.*)

SPENCE: (*Takes the pill.*) I know what you're going to say. "You're beginning to look fatter already." (*She laughs merrily and hugs him.*) You're going to make me spill the water.

CHRISTINE: (*Releases him. Takes glass and puts it on tray.*) What else?

SPENCE: Well, I'm going to cut out the damn smoking and drinking and that ought to fix up the old body. (*Rises, crosses Right.*) Then I've got to go up to school and make peace with old Hasbrook and Crowley. But the other things are going to be a hell of a lot harder to do.

CHRISTINE: What are they?

SPENCE: (*Sits chair Right.*) I've got to do something about the guys and my Gram, Christine. I'm going to be honest with you about Gram – it's going to be hard. I miss her a hell of a lot. But she's dead, Christine. She's dead – and you can tell yourself that and you can accept it, and maybe I'm a little selfish about it, but you know that no other living soul is talking with her or having fun with her. She didn't ditch you. She died. But the guys are different, Christine. They're not dead. They're over in the lot playing baseball. They're still horsing around up in the park. I don't suppose they can really help what's happened because that's the way it is. I've said some pretty lousy things to them, Christine, and I don't want it to be that way. (*He pauses. He is near tears.*) God damn it – I hate being black, Christine. I hate it. I hate it. I hate the hell out of it.

CHRISTINE: (*Crosses to him, holds him.*) Ssh!

SPENCE: I'm sorry I said that, Christine.

CHRISTINE: It's all right, Spence. You don't have to explain to me. (*She releases him, but still holds his hand.*)

SPENCE: And I've got to cut out this goddamn crying. Everything makes me cry. I don't understand it. I was watching television the other day – a damn soap opera – and started crying like a baby. That's damn peculiar.

CHRISTINE: It's not so peculiar as you think.

SPENCE: There's just one more thing, Christine.

CHRISTINE: What is it?

SPENCE: I don't know whether I should tell you or not.

CHRISTINE: Sure you can tell me.

SPENCE: How are you so sure? You don't even know what it is yet.

CHRISTINE: I'll take the risk.

SPENCE: You promise you won't say anything about it to anybody?

CHRISTINE: I won't mention it to a soul.

SPENCE: No matter what it is?

CHRISTINE: I've already said I won't tell it, haven't I?

SPENCE: Well, I want to sleep with a girl, Christine. (*Christine turns away laughing.*) What's the matter with you?

CHRISTINE: Nothing. I just swallowed wrong.

SPENCE: Yeh!

CHRISTINE: (*Turns to him.*) Yeh! And many more of them right back at you. Who's the lucky girl?

SPENCE: Aw! Christine. You know I haven't got any girl in mind. I think about it quite often, but I can't think of anybody. I suppose you think that sounds pretty horny to be thinking of it all the time?

CHRISTINE: (*Turns away.*) No, I wouldn't say that.

SPENCE: You wouldn't?

CHRISTINE: No, I wouldn't.

SPENCE: You know, Christine. You're a funny Joe. To look at you no one would think that somebody could talk to you like this.

CHRISTINE: (*Quite dryly, turns to him.*) Thanks.

SPENCE: Have you had much experience, Christine?

CHRISTINE: Enough.

SPENCE: Offhand – how much experience would you say you've had?

CHRISTINE: Now that's the kind of question it's every woman's right to leave unanswered.

SPENCE: You think that's a pretty nosey question?

CHRISTINE: I not only think it's a nosey question. I know it is.

SPENCE: O.K. (*Rises. Crosses to below bed. Christine sits chair Right. Pause.*) Would you say, offhand, that I was trying to rush things, Christine?

CHRISTINE: How do you mean?

SPENCE: (*Crossing Down Right.*) You'd just as soon we talked about something else, wouldn't you?

CHRISTINE: I just didn't understand what you meant, that's all.

SPENCE: (*Crossing to Center.*) Well, I mean about my age and all. Do you realize that I'm going on eighteen and have never slept with a girl?

CHRISTINE: That's terrible – isn't it? (*Turns away.*)

SPENCE: It sure as hell is. Hell, I'm practically a virgin. And you know I was thinking when I was sick, supposing I died. Supposing I just passed out now and died. (*Indicates imaginary body on floor.*) Why, I'd regret that I hadn't slept with anybody for the rest of my life practically.

CHRISTINE: I guess that would be pretty terrible – wouldn't it?

SPENCE: I think that you're having a hell of a good time laughing at me.

CHRISTINE: I most certainly am not.

SPENCE: You sure as hell are. You've got a sneaky laugh line around your whole mouth.

CHRISTINE: (*Turns to him.*) Spence – I'm not laughing. I wouldn't laugh at you when you're telling me things like this. If I'm doing anything I'm remembering, and I might be just smiling a little bit at the memory, but I'm not laughing at you.

SPENCE: You really honestly don't think that its peculiar or anything?

CHRISTINE: How could anything so natural be peculiar?

SPENCE: That's a funny thing for you to say.

CHRISTINE: Why is it so funny, might I ask?

SPENCE: (*Sits on foot of bed.*) Well, I'm pretty sure, although I've never asked her, that Mom would give me a swat for my pains if –

CHRISTINE: (*Rises, crosses to him.*) And what makes you think that your mother and I should have the same ideas?

SPENCE: Well – you're both older than I am.

CHRISTINE: Well, I'm not anywhere near as old as your mother. I might be a widow, but I'm a young widow, and I'm not through yet by a long shot.

SPENCE: I didn't mean –

CHRISTINE: I know exactly what you meant. Just remember you're no Tiny Tim yourself.

SPENCE: I didn't mean what you thought I meant at all. I just meant that you seem to understand a lot of things. Aw! Hell – I don't mean that. I mean you seem to understand me – and I'm grateful. That's all.

CHRISTINE: (*Crosses to chair Left. After a pause.*) Well, we've done enough talking for one afternoon. I've got to go.

SPENCE: Christine!

CHRISTINE: (*Turning around.*) What is it now?

SPENCE: (*Pause.*) Nothing.

CHRISTINE: (*Crossing to Center.*) Nothing is what you ask for, nothing is what you'll get.

SPENCE: (*Rises.*) Christine! –
(*She stops.*) I'd appreciate it if you don't turn around.

CHRISTINE: Why?

SPENCE: (*Standing behind her.*) Because I'm going to ask you something and If you're going to laugh at me I'd just as soon you weren't laughing in my face.

CHRISTINE: I won't laugh.

SPENCE: Well, would you mind not turning around just the same?

CHRISTINE: All right.

SPENCE: Well – I don't know quite how to say it. (*Pause.*) Do you like me, Christine?

CHRISTINE: I certainly do.

SPENCE: No kidding?

CHRISTINE: No kidding.

SPENCE: I was sure hoping you weren't. Because I like you too, Christine.

CHRISTINE: Thank you.

SPENCE: Well, I know that liking doesn't mean loving – but I kind of thought – that since – well – you're lonely, aren't you, Christine?

CHRISTINE: I've been lonely for a long time now, boy.

SPENCE: Well – in case you didn't know, I'm lonely too, Christine – and I know that you're older than I am and I know it makes a lot of difference.

CHRISTINE: I have to go, Spence.

SPENCE: But what I'm lacking in age, Christine, I sure make up for in loneliness, and so we do have that much in common. Don't we, Christine?

CHRISTINE: Yes.

SPENCE: So maybe – if you stayed, Christine – since things are like I said they were – we might find a little happiness together. I don't mean for forever or anything like that – but could you call and say you couldn't make it?

CHRISTINE: You know you're very young, Spence, and you could be very foolish too. You know that – don't you?

SPENCE: Yes, Christine. I know.

CHRISTINE: And I could be very foolish to listen to you.

SPENCE: I know, Christine.

CHRISTINE: (*Turns to him.*) It's funny. I have to look at you, because I can't believe that you said what you just said. You said, that since we were both lonely maybe – just for an afternoon – we could find happiness together. You know that so soon?

SPENCE: Yes, Christine.

CHRISTINE: You see, I didn't laugh. I ain't laughing at all. I'll try to come back. I'll try. (*She gets the tray from the bureau and goes to the door.*)

SPENCE: You know where the phone is. If you can't come back, Christine, you don't need to come up and tell me. Just go. But if you can, there's a bell downstairs on the table that mother uses to call us to meals. Would you ring it – if you can?

CHRISTINE: I'll try. (*She exits.*)

SPENCE: (*Crossing Down Right, then to door; listens.*) Why in hell is she taking so long?

(*Sound of hand bell off Right. Spence crosses slowly to window, pulls shade down as lights fade.*)

Talking Pictures
By Horton Foote

Katie Bell, 16; Estaquio, 17

Like most of Horton Foote's plays, *Talking Pictures* is set in the fictitious Texas town of Harrison. The year is 1929, eventful in part because the new rage in American entertainment was about to land in small-town U.S.A. – "talking pictures." The play concerns Myra Tolliver, a single mother who makes her living playing piano for the silent movies at the local theater. Myra and her son, Pete, rent rooms in the Jackson house. Mr. Jackson is a railroad engineer. Myra fears she'll lose her job playing piano at the theater, no longer needed, when the talkies start coming to Harrison. The loss of her job would threaten her independence and could result in Pete's distant father taking him away from Myra. Although the events take place in a small town, the ideas are universal. Such is the case in all of Mr. Foote's plays. Perhaps it is this minute focus that brings such clear and specific value to the character's voices. Here the small town's narrow-mindedness is often racist as characters speak of the local blacks and Mexicans in dismissive and caustic tones. However, Katie Bell Jackson, the youngest daughter of the house, is more worldly curious than most.

In the scene below, Katie Bell is given a second opportunity to interact with young Estaquio, a Mexican boy who has come to Harrison with his preacher father in the hopes of starting a Spanish speaking church for local Mexicans.

KATIE BELL: Hello. (*Vesta goes into the house.*) What are you doing here?

ESTAQUIO: I've come to say goodbye. I'm going back to Mexico.

KATIE BELL: Oh, well. Goodbye.

ESTAQUIO: And I've come to invite you to visit me in Mexico one day.

KATIE BELL: Thank you, but I wouldn't dare go there.

ESTAQUIO: Why?

KATIE BELL: It's too far away and besides, II wouldn't know a word anybody was saying.

ESTAQUIO: You could learn to speak Spanish –

KATIE BELL: I guess I could. I almost took it in school. I took Latin instead because Vesta did. Did you and your Papa get your church started?

ESTAQUIO: No.

KATIE BELL: I didn't ask the other day what kind of church it was.

ESTAQUIO: Baptist.

KATIE BELL: We are all Methodists.

ESTAQUIO: Are you? We Baptists believe in total immersion and we have no crosses in our church –

KATIE BELL: Is that so?

ESTAQUIO: I hope to be a preacher one day –

KATIE BELL: Baptist?

ESTAQUIO: Certainly – Jesus was a Baptist, you know –

KATIE BELL: Was He?

ESTAQUIO: Yes.

KATIE BELL: I never knew that. When you preach are you going to preach in English or Spanish?

ESTAQUIO: In Spanish. Jehova es mi salvador, nada me faltara.

KATIE BELL: What does that mean?

ESTAQUIO: The Lord is my Shepherd, I shall not want.

KATIE BELL: Oh, go on –

(Pete comes into the yard. He is 14. He has a suitcase.)

[PETE: Hello, Katie Bell.]

[KATIE BELL: Hi.]

[PETE: Is my Mom here?]

[KATIE BELL: She's still at the picture show.]

(He puts the suitcase on the porch. He starts out.)

[PETE: I'm going to find my mom. *(He leaves.)*]

KATIE BELL: *(Whispering.)* His Mommy and Daddy are divorced. She's a grass widow. Do you know what that means?

ESTAQUIO: No.

KATIE BELL: Well, if you're a widow your husband is dead, but if you're a grass widow he's still alive.

ESTAQUIO: I'm going to be a Baptist preacher, too. My papa may let me start preaching soon. I'm practicing now. My first sermon is going to be about sin. That's a terrible thing, you know, sin is.

KATIE BELL: Yes, I expect so –

ESTAQUIO: Sin makes you drink and makes you gamble and go

wrong. I wrestle with the devil all the time.

KATIE BELL: Do you?

ESTAQUIO: All the time. I talk rough to him. I tell him to go away and leave me alone. The devil got hold of my Mama, you know.

KATIE BELL: Did he?

ESTAQUIO: Oh, yes. Got hold of her and wouldn't let her go. My Papa prayed and I prayed but he won out. She ran off and left Papa and me. She hated church. Hated the Bible. Hated hymns. Hated Jesus. That was just the devil making her say that. I'm going to pray. Bow your head. Dious, dame valor para testificar a esta muchacha y su familia la palabra de dious. Y que sean vendicidos. Tambien por medio de tu vendicion, ellos logren sus metas. Te pido SEÑOR, que con ternura ella se fije en mi. AMEN. Don't I pray good? Papa taught me to do that. What does your Papa do?

KATIE BELL: He's an engineer. He's been bumped.

ESTAQUIO: What does that mean?

KATIE BELL: It means when you work for the railroad when someone who has more seniority than you do wants your job they can have it.

ESTAQUIO: Is he out of a job?

KATIE BELL: No, but now he has to bump someone and take their job.

ESTAQUIO: Maybe he'll bump someone in Mexico.

KATIE BELL: Oh, I don't think so.

ESTAQUIO: We don't know where my Mama is. We saw her on the street one day in Mexico City, but when we went up to her she said she didn't even know who we were. She told us to go away and mind our own business. But we didn't listen to her. We stayed right there beside her on the street corner praying, and then we went on. She never was a true Baptist, Papa said. Not in her heart. She used to slip off and go to confession all the time.

Thin Air: Tales From A Revolution
By Lynne Alvarez

Anya, 16; Johnny, early 20s

Lynne Alvarez' *Thin Air: Tales From A Revolution* is a boldly theatrical play set against the tumultuous backdrop of a fictitious South American country in the midst of a revolution. The story concerns Anya, the daughter of American Alexander Young and Hilda Inez Santa Maria de Young, a well-born South American. Anya's family came to this part of the world to focus on Alexander's research of cultural music. During their time in the provinces, Alexander's secret political involvement separates him from the family. While searching for her father, Anya is abducted at the gates of the Candelaria (the local prison), never to be reunited with her parents. Through the course of the play, which moves back and forth in time, we see Hilda and Alexander in South America and in the United States piecing together the veiled details of Anya's abduction. Their efforts are both aided and confused by their involvement with General Juan Lescos Villanueva, a powerful player in the revolution. We also see Anya in prison, grappling for answers about her father and clinging to life. The themes of justice, conviction in one's beliefs, and cultural conflicts or race and class, give form to a unique exploration that is both poetic and dangerous. In the two scenes that follow, we see Anya and Johnny, a guard at the Candelaria.

This scene details their initial meeting.

◆ ◆ ◆ ◆

The Prison: Some guests at the cocktail party become vendors, beggars, relatives waiting outside the prison. They hassle Anya from time to time. The little girl is with her brother. She is slowly removing the flowers which cover him. Beneath each flower is a red wound. She makes a pile of the flowers next to her.

Lights up. Anya comes running in. She is in her school uniform and is carrying some books. She goes to the gate of the prison, looks for someone to talk to, tries desperately to see inside.

ANYA: Hello?! Hello?!

JOHNNY: (*Walking in on his usual tour.*) What do you want?

ANYA: My papa. He's in here. His name is Alexander Bertram Young.

JOHNNY: Don't know him.

ANYA: He was brought in. Today. Look. I know he's here. My neighbor followed the police. They grabbed him off the street and dragged him here. I swear.

JOHNNY: You can't stand here. Move back.

ANYA: Maybe you could find him. He's . . . he's not old, but he looks old. His hair is grey and he wears glasses. He's taller than you and . . . and I don't know what he was wearing but . . .

JOHNNY: I'm sorry.

ANYA: Papa! Papa!

JOHNNY: You can't stand here yelling like that.

ANYA: He'll know my voice. Is he in the courtyard? (*She strains to see.*)

JOHNNY: (*Steps between her and the gate.*) I'm sorry, girl.

ANYA: He's an American. He'd be easy to spot. He's an American. I'm sure they made a mistake. They can't arrest him.

JOHNNY: Maybe he stole something. Maybe he killed someone. Even Americans do that.

ANYA: No. Not him. It's a mistake. He's a musician. A composer. He doesn't even have a penknife. Please.

JOHNNY: I'll be right back. What was his name?

ANYA: Not was. Is. His name is Alexander Bertram Young.

JOHNNY: I'm doing you a favor, you know. (*Johnny exits.*)

(*Anya paces. She notices the little girl.*)

[ANYA: What's wrong?]

[(*The little girl clutches her dead brother tighter.*)]

[LITTLE GIRL: He's asleep. He's my brother.]

[ANYA: Is he hurt?]

[LITTLE GIRL: They covered him with red flowers from their magic wands.]

[ANYA: Those aren't flowers, little girl.]

[LITTLE GIRL: They are too!]

JOHNNY: There's an American here.

ANYA: Is it him?

JOHNNY: I've already told you too much.

ANYA: Why is he in jail? What did he do?

JOHNNY: I don't know.

ANYA: Then let him out!

JOHNNY: I can't let him out.

ANYA: But he's in for no reason.

JOHNNY: Well he can't get out 'til we know why he's in. There's nothing I can do. Well, maybe you can give something. What can you give?

ANYA: I don't know.

JOHNNY: Do you have money?

ANYA: Why? What's it to you? Oh – I know.

JOHNNY: What?!

ANYA: You want a bribe. You people always do.

JOHNNY: You stupid girl, it's not for me. There are other people to pay off. I've seen it done.

ANYA: (*Goes to the gate.*) Papa! Papa!

JOHNNY: I told you. You can't do that.

ANYA: It'll keep his spirits up, if he knows I'm here. You tell him!

JOHNNY: (*Roughly jerks her away.*) No. Shut up. (*She does.*) They'll come out and put you in too. You're rich. I can tell. You expect everything to go your way. (*He hands her a handkerchief, she blows her nose.*)

ANYA: Thank you.

JOHNNY: And that uniform. Where do you go to school? I don't recognize it.

ANYA: The American School.

JOHNNY: It's a rich school, isn't it? Mostly foreigners.

ANYA: I'm not a foreigner. I was born here. My mother's from here.

JOHNNY: Well go to your mother and use your money to get your father out of jail. That's how it's done.

ANYA: My mother's in Spain.

JOHNNY: Well there's nothing I can do.

ANYA: You're from the provinces. I can tell by your accent. (*Looks at him closely.*) And you're only a boy. (*Disdainfully.*) There's obviously nothing a boy from the provinces can do. You probably still ride a donkey to work.

JOHNNY: You know if I really wanted to . . .

ANYA: What?

JOHNNY: You're spoiled.

ANYA: What would you do? Go ahead. I dare you. (*He doesn't do anything.*) See! So. You won't help at all.

JOHNNY: I don't pity you. If that's what you expect. I know girls who already have two children at your age, good mothers, hardworking wives. Go away from here. Go pull all those little strings you were born holding. You must know someone in the government. Get out of here!

(*Johnny marches off smartly. Lights dim except over the little girl.*)

◆ ◆ ◆ ◆

Anya, 16; Johnny, early 20s

Later, Johnny reveals the conflict he faces in his role in the revolution.

They move forward. The line of prisoners moves offstage. We see the pattern of clouds move across the back of the stage. Some birds. They are in a park. He throws her on a bench.

JOHNNY: There. Sit! See. I can talk to you like a dog. (*He looks around.*) Do you remember me?

ANYA: No.

JOHNNY: You asked me if I still rode a donkey to work.

ANYA: I don't remember. What do you want?

JOHNNY: I'm a man. You're a woman. What do you think I want?

ANYA: Do what you want then. I don't care.

JOHNNY: Have there been so many?

ANYA: There haven't been any. I just don't care.

JOHNNY: So, you're a virgin? (*She doesn't say anything.*) You can't fool me, you know. I can tell the difference. (*She doesn't answer him.*) I'm not a virgin.

ANYA: Who cares?

JOHNNY: Stupid girl. Don't you know anything. If you're a virgin, I'll marry you. If you're not, I'll send you to a whorehouse.

ANYA: What?

JOHNNY: I don't think they should kill you. Idiot. I saved your life. Yeah. They thought I was going to take you out and rape you and cut your throat. Didn't you? That was pretty good.

ANYA: And you want to marry me?

JOHNNY: Sure. Only if you're a virgin.

ANYA: Why? You don't even know who I am.

JOHNNY: Sure I do. Your mother was in Spain. I was at the gate when you were looking for your father. You said you went to the American school. I know who you are. I thought of you over and over, but I never thought I would see you again. Girls like you don't look at me twice. (*He touches her hair.*) Girls like you with light skin and light hair and read foreign magazines and wear pretty clothes. But you're spoiled.

ANYA: You're right. I'm really spoiled. I can't cook. I can't sew. It would be completely stupid to marry me. I'd cry all the time. Why don't you just let me go.

JOHNNY: You'll have pretty babies. I want lots of them. My mother'd be pleased. She'd like someone else in the house. My sisters moved two towns away and she complains she hardly sees them. She complains a lot! She has arthritis, so she bends way over when she walks. She complains she knows every crack in the floor better than her own daughters 'cause that's all she sees. (*He laughs. Anya doesn't.*) You could give her massages. You could read to her too. She can't read. I can read, but I won't have time. I'll fish like my father. He was a good fisherman, but he bought a boat with a partner and they had terrible fights. My father had a bad temper and hands like hammers. People were afraid of him. Me too. So finally someone shot him in the back. I still own half the boat and the partner's old now. He had no sons. So I have something to go back to. I'll walk in with a wife. A beautiful wife. Can you imagine? We'll have a good life, as long as you're a virgin. Otherwise I can't promise you anything. If you start out with more than one man, you'll always want more than one man. I wouldn't stand for that.

ANYA: I don't want to go with you.

JOHNNY: Do you want to die from a helicopter?

ANYA: No.

JOHNNY: You'll be safe with me. There's only 500 in my town. We don't let strangers in. My cousin's brother-in-law is mayor. We all call each other "cousin" whether we're related or not. We probably are. Not many new people around. That's why I left. But now with a new wife – it'll be different. There's dances in the park and you can swim in the river – that is – when I take you.

ANYA: Why get married? Why not just have a good time . . . for a while. You know.

JOHNNY: Once you have babies you won't think so much about leaving.

ANYA: I don't want babies.

JOHNNY: You can't stop that.

ANYA: I'll hate you.

JOHNNY: I saved your life. You won't hate me.

ANYA: It'll be so lonely for me, you know. And my parents – they'll think I'm dead.

JOHNNY: I know that. But I want you. Now kiss me.

ANYA: No.

JOHNNY: Don't act like that.

ANYA: You can kiss me, if you want. I won't yell or anything.

JOHNNY: No. I want you to kiss me. (*He slaps her.*)

ANYA: That's how you treat a wife?

JOHNNY: Oh, yes. Now kiss me.

ANYA: Fine. I'll kiss you, I'll fuck you, I'll lick your boots if you want me to, I'll clean your ass and I'll have babies and start the world all over again. That's what you want isn't it! (*She kisses him on the cheek.*)

JOHNNY: (*He grabs her.*) Who taught you to talk that way?

ANYA: Some guy in jail.

JOHNNY: If he taught you anything else, I'll know. (*He kisses her on the mouth.*) This is the best thing I've done in my life! I'll treat you like a queen. You'll see. I'll get you a dress and some sandals. We'll get my things. But quiet. If you talk to anyone but me I'll have to shoot you.

ANYA: I'm cold.

JOHNNY: Here. (*He gives her his jacket.*) Wait 'til Carmen sees I've run off with you. I'm glad I'll be out of reach. She'd tear my eyes out.

ANYA: Who's Carmen?

JOHNNY: A girl. Let's go. (*He pushes her.*) Move!

Troubled Waters
By Brian Kral

Bet, mid-teens; J.D., mid-teens

In *Troubled Waters*, Brian Kral uses as his jumping off point a series of newspaper articles he read that dealt with hunters converging in a "mercy kill" of deer. Set in the Florida Everglades, the play centers around two brothers, J.D. and Michael, and their sister, Sandra, and their friend, Bet, an American-Indian girl. After recent droughts and later flooding weaken the deer population, government officials decide to kill the undernourished deer in order to save healthy deer. When there is a large public outcry against this, the children are forced to consider the moral and ecological issues raised by such a "mercy kill."

In Scene 7 of the play, Bet and J.D. attempt to save a bird that has been caught in a trap.

J.D.: Can we save 'er?
(*Slight pause.*)
BET: She looks pretty mangled, J.D., I don't know. How'd ya get 'er outta that trap?
J.D. I just opened it. I was walkin' by and heard 'er wing flappin' in the brush, and I opened it and took 'er out.
BET: I'm surprised. Those things're stronger'na dickens. And mean! See here? The teeth on that thing snapped clean through 'er wing, that's the problem. I don't know if we can fix 'er. Or if she'll stay put long enough for it to mend. That's the problem.
J.D. She's sure shakin'.
BET: She's scared. Maybe in shock, too. Might be better to kill 'er.
(*Slight pause.*)
J.D. How could that be better?
BET: Stop 'er sufferin'.
J.D. (*Looks down at the bird.*) She ain't shakin' no more.
BET: Nope. I think she's gone. (*She folds a towel around the bird.*) Ya did what you could. She was just too darn mangled. That was the problem.
J.D. Aren't traps against the law inside a the park?

BET: Most places, yeah. But who's gonna come out here lookin' for a couple game poachers with illegal traps?

J.D. I would. And Michael would too, I s'pose.

BET: That's one a the things they pay your brother for, sure. And when he finds a trap, I bet he busts it up good. But that's a whole lot diff'rnt from findin' its owners.

J.D. It ain't fair.

BET: Never said it was fair, I'm sayin' it's how it is – leastways out here. Things die, or get themselves killed, without ever meanin' to, while other things live and don't deserve to, like them poachers. If this bird hadn't come pokin' around that trap, she'da likely been got by some other animal. It's natural.

J.D. It still ain't fair. Mother Nature didn't put that trap out.

BET: No. but she's got other traps. And she gives all a her animals defenses against things, to even it out.

J.D. This bird didn't have no chance to use any defenses far as I can see.

BET: That's true, J.D. But it's dead all the same. And wishin' it was some other way'll only make ya unhappy.
(Slight pause.)

J.D. What about the deer? What kinda defenses do they got?

BET: Against hunters? Not a whole heckuva lot.

J.D. So shouldn't we do somethin' to help 'em?

BET: Like what?

J.D. I dunno. But that's why my sister's here. She's gonna try, at least.

BET: This the same sister that chased us off?

J.D. She was mad at Michael. *And* me. And maybe she was right. What d'*you* think?
(Pause. Bet takes on a mysterious quality, as though preparing to describe something supernatural.)

BET: Well, I can tell ya what the Indians did. They lived with the deer, and respected 'em. Indians weren't afraid to kill a deer. Though some of 'em would say a little prayer beforehand, askin' the deer to forgive them. But the important part was that they put that deer to good use – ev'ry bit a meat or patch a fur had some purpose to those people. And when they were done, they'd take the bones that were left over, and they'd give 'em a little ceremony by returnin' 'em to the river, which's where they'd come from.

J.D. What good did that do 'em? They were already dead.

BET: Yes . . . and no. See, the water's where they'd *come* from . . . and so the water was where they could come from *again*. Those bones'd get mixed around, and start all over.

J.D. Makin' a new deer? (*Bet nods seriously.*) How are they gonna become a new one, when the bones are always gonna be in the river.

BET: How d'ya know the bones are there? And where *are* all the bones of dead things? If the bones just stayed where they are when somethin' died, wouldn't the whole world be covered by 'em by now? You got bones from the beginnin' of time, J.D. . . . where'd they all go?

J.D. They're makin' new things? (*Bet nods seriously.*) Damn. How'd they do that ceremony?

BET: Well, they'd take them bones . . . (*She looks around, finds a square of cloth.*) and they'd wrap 'em in an oilcloth, so's the moisture wouldn't get to 'em too soon. Then they'd carry the bones to the river, usually late at night, when the moon was dim, so no ghosts or spirits'd see 'em. They'd hold the bones close to their chests, protectin' 'em, and makin' sure there was heat all around 'em, keepin' those bones warm. When they got to the riverbank, they'd kneel down real quiet, and sweep away leaves and twigs with the flat a their hand. They'd look into the water, to see it was clear . . .

(*Bet dramatically enacts each stage of the ceremony. Behind them, the dream-deer appears.*)

. . . and they'd unwrap those bones cautious-like. They'd hold them out, straight in front of 'em. And they'd lower them into the water, without sayin' a word . . . (*She looks at J.D., who is captivated.*) Last they'd take a sprinkle of stuff from their pouch – ground-up antler, dried pieces a hide, maybe even a handful of fur, see? – and they'd drop these over the water,

just to get things goin'. Then they'd hurry back to their home,
knowin' they'd got some strong magic workin'.
(*The deer moves slowly and gracefully behind them.*)

J.D. And that'd make a new deer?
(*Bet nods. From the wall, she takes down a ceremonial
headpiece representing a deer, puts it on and begins moving
around the room as a deer-dancer, while behind her the
dream-deer continues in its own representational movements,
in counterpoint to Bet's.*)

BET: Ev'ry year the deer would return. And that's how the Indians
and the deer managed to live together so long.

Valentin and Valentina
By Mikhail Roschin; Translated by Irene Arn Vacchina and Edward Hastings

Valentin, 18, Valentina, 18

Set in Russia prior to the overthrow of Communism, *Valentin and Valentina* is a modern-day variation of the tale of *Romeo and Juliet*. Love is the central theme as two young people confront their families' class prejudices. Along the way, the lovers also become caught up in the all-consuming work principle, until love and ambition collide.

Here Valentin and Valentina speak of their love for each other.

VALENTIN: Do you want to lay down?

VALENTINA: (*Corrects his grammar.*) Not lay, lie . . . wait, Val . . .

VALENTIN: Why are you like this? Tonight is . . . I missed you so. It seems as if I haven't seen you in a hundred years . . . You know, I understood: love is when not seeing each other is impossible, the agony just eats you up. It seems, without seeing her one more day you won't be able to breathe . . . Yes? For you, too? And another thing I noticed: the only time that I don't think of you is when I am with you. Otherwise – all the time, every minute.

VALENTINA: I fall asleep, I wake up – only you . . . I walk, eat, sit at lectures . . . for a long time I haven't heard a thing at lectures.

VALENTIN: Exactly, exactly . . . It's so fantastic that we met. Actually I always imagined . . . although like all the guys I used to laugh, what's all this love, nonsense! But that's how it is! That's it! It is!

VALENTINA: Wait, Valechka. It is so . . . it terrifies me.

VALENTIN: Do you remember how I couldn't even touch you?

VALENTINA: And I wished every minute that you'd at least take me by the hand . . . and it was I who started it?

VALENTIN: Of course, at the movies, remember? Actually, I had nothing to do with it!

VALENTINA: Aha, granny is right. She says: men have become like women, and women like men.

VALENTIN: Now, now, and who gave you the apple first? I'll never forget it! Remember that morning? You kept walking slower and slower, swinging your little . . . bookbag, looking back at me . . .

VALENTINA: And you came up and said: 'Miss, would you like an apple?' Just like the Serpent.

VALENTIN: No. dumbbell . . . Like Paris.

VALENTINA: See, we already have a long history! We've recalled that first meeting a hundred times.

VALENTIN: And it's never boring.

VALENTINA: Aha, someone said: lovers never bore each other, because they speak only of themselves.

VALENTIN: La Rochefoucauld said it. What an edition of his works has just come out! Where do you get money for books? What a library Sergei Sergeevich has!

VALENTINA: You become a professor, you will too.

VALENTIN: I want to be everybody: a welder, a baker, a poet, a physicist, a trolley driver, a shoemaker.

VALENTINA: You're like a little boy!

VALENTIN: And a professor also! Alechka!!

VALENTINA: Just a minute, wait . . . And have you always met girls that way?

VALENTIN: I? Actually, I never met any.

VALENTINA: Oh! Swear that you never had any romances!

VALENTIN: I've sworn already, what's the matter with you?

VALENTINA: Swear again! Some Lenochka, in that tourist camp, this Katiusha, your neighbor! Well?

VALENTIN: Katiusha? That's a laugh!

VALENTINA: And that beauty Dina from your class?

VALENTIN: Well Dina! – Dina is like one of the family, what's wrong with you?

VALENTINA: No, no, look me in the eye! You libertine, you're nothing but a Don Juan, don't laugh . . . If I hear any more about this Dina, I don't know what I'll do!

VALENTIN: Oh, Alia, stop it! What Dina, what Katiusha? Actually, I don't see anyone. All the girls have disappeared from the city, there's no one, except you.

VALENTINA: Don't, wait.

VALENTIN: Alia!

VALENTINA: Wait dear . . .

VALENTIN: Well, Alia . . .

VALENTINA: You only think of one thing.

VALENTIN: Yeah, well?

VALENTINA: And what if something happens?

VALENTIN: (*Carefree, boyishly.*) So we'll have a boy, so what?

VALENTINA: You – nut.

VALENTIN: We'll buy him a railroad.

VALENTINA: I'd rather jump off a bridge.

VALENTIN: Alia!

VALENTINA: And college?

VALENTIN: (*Same carefree tone.*) To hell with college!

VALENTINA: We have nothing.

VALENTIN: I'll go to work.

VALENTINA: I can't allow you because of me to . . .

VALENTIN: (*Seriously now.*) Listen, Alia, I'll die for you, if I have to! Don't you understand?

VALENTINA: You really love me?

VALENTIN: Oh, I don't know how to say it . . .

VALENTINA: And what if it all ends? You know, according to Freud, love lasts about four years.

VALENTIN: Freud, who? To hell with him.

VALENTINA: First love always ends badly.

VALENTIN: First love does not end ever . . . Alia, Alia . . .

VALENTINA: (*Whispering.*) I am asking you, wait . . .

VALENTIN: (*Also whispering.*) Let me . . . this is all so distasteful. (*She quickly dresses. Valentin gets his coat. Valentina runs out. Valentin follows and they are once again in the street. Frost. Street lights. Roar of the city.*)

VALENTIN: We've got to get the license. Make it official. Then at least we won't have to hide, lie, spoil everything.

VALENTINA: The most degrading part is the lying.

VALENTIN: Don't be afraid! We have our whole life ahead of us! We'll go away somewhere, we'll work in the same school, you'll torture kids with math, and me with history. And then I'll write my thesis.

VALENTINA: Oh, it's so unknown!

VALENTIN: We can do it!

VALENTINA: No – no, it is all because of how I am. I am old-fashioned. One should take everything lightly and simply. You have to live, be happy and not think. And I have tortured both of us . . . I want to be with you always, to work with you, and of course to have a home and children. I'd make it all so perfect. I know how, granny taught me everything. Maybe I wasn't brought up right? Maybe I wasn't brought up right? Maybe I'm just a petty bourgeois? But I can't behave this way! This is degrading, it's shameful! We give a girl a ruble to leave the house and pretend that she doesn't understand anything. And later she'll do the same thing? You say: love! But because of love people kill each other, become like animals, doesn't that happen? I want to be a person, I want to be proud of my love, I want to carry it like a crown on my head, and not like a cursed cross on my shoulders. I don't want it to crush us! Forgive me.

VALENTIN: Don't talk nonsense. I'll think of something . . . I'll ask the guys . . .

VALENTINA: But I can't be any other way, you see . . .

VALENTIN: I'll do everything to make it easy for you.

VALENTINA: You can send me away, leave me.

VALENTIN: Alia!

VALENTINA: I won't be hurt, I'll understand.

VALENTIN: Do you love me?

VALENTINA: (*In a tired voice.*) Yes.

VALENTIN: And I love you. Tomorrow at six? By the small metro?

VALENTINA: Yes . . . No, you'd better call me first.

VALENTIN: (*Alarmed.*) What? Why?

VALENTINA: Forgive me! Forgive me for being as I am. (*She runs off.*)

VALENTIN: (*A cry of despair.*) Valia!

Welcome Home Jacko
By Mustapha Matura

Gail, 20-25; Zippy, 17-21

Mustapha Matura, perhaps the leading dramatist of West Indian origin, wrote *Welcome Home Jacko* after visiting a community youth center in Sheffield, England. The center was a place for young people to socialize apart from the pangs of social oppression and racism. The play, set in just such a center, concerns a group of young people struggling for a Black identity. As the four young West Indians interact in the Club, exploring their place in the world, they assert their beliefs. Sandy, the white girl who manages the club, is preparing to welcome home Jacko, who has spent the last five years in prison for raping a girl.

In the scene below, Gail, a young black woman from London, arrives to interview for work at the club. Here she encounters Zippy, a West Indian, in Rastafarian robe. Zippy is a regular at the club and a devout Rastafarian.

ZIPPY: (*Jumping, sings.*) By de water of Babylon . . . Cha
  (*A girl, Gail, enters. She is black, attractive (twenty to twenty-five) and is wearing a jacket, skirt and jumper.*)
GAIL: Hello.
ZIPPY: Yes?
GAIL: I came to see Sandy.
ZIPPY: Yes, she a gone out but she left a message she say she en go be long ter wait fer she.
GAIL: Yes, I'm a bit late, I couldn't find the place.
ZIPPY: Yes, Cha take a seat, she a come soon.
GAIL: (*Sits.*) Thank you, it looks nice.
ZIPPY: It aright, it have office upstairs you ar want to see it?
GAIL: No, I better wait till Sandy comes.
ZIPPY: Yea, you a come ter work?
GAIL: I hope so, it's up to Sandy if she likes me.
ZIPPY: Cha, Sandy cool she a like you she a like everybody, you en help she out.
GAIL: Yes.

Scenes for One Woman and One Man **123**

ZIPPY: What you a do?

GAIL: I . . . Lots of things, try to keep you busy most of all. Are you the only one here?

ZIPPY: No de rest a guys upstairs dey look fer dem robes, you like it? (*Stands.*) It a genuine Ethiopian robe.

GAIL: Yes, it's very nice.

ZIPPY: Sandy a make a dem fer we. She a cool, you a ask she, she make you one.

GAIL: Yes, I'll ask her, so what other rooms do you have?

ZIPPY: Cha, not much, we a have office an phone upstairs, toilet over dey.

GAIL: One?

ZIPPY: Nar two, one for de girls.

GAIL: Yes.

ZIPPY: An in de back dey it a have a room for discos.

GAIL: Ah, I like dancing, how often do you . . . ?

ZIPPY: Cha, not too often, it a some time one week, some time two weeks, not steady. Whey you from?

GAIL: London.

ZIPPY: But yer people black.

GAIL: Yes.

ZIPPY: Cha, me know dat me take one look at yer me know yer people a dem black. You is a Rastafarian?

GAIL: No, I don't think so, not that I have anything against it, I just don't know anything about it.

ZIPPY: Me tell yer, me explain everything not Marcus him a hypocrite.

GAIL: Who's Marcus?

ZIPPY: Him a upstairs. Yer see Rastafarian is a man who believe in de Bible, all peace an love an him a believe in Emperor Haile Selassie to be de Lion a Judah, de King of Kings and Lord of Lords.

GAIL: Yes?

ZIPPY: Dat is something eh, dat is Rasta man, him belief. Yes, an all white people all a dem, dem a genuine hypocrite dem.

GAIL: Yes I see.

ZIPPY: See dat what Rasta man believe.

GAIL: And you're a Rasta man?

ZIPPY: Cha all a we a Rasta an all Rasta man believe in him dread locks.

GAIL: Yes, the hair.

ZIPPY: Dat not him hair, dat him dread locks.

GAIL: I see, so tell me what sort of things you do here?

ZIPPY: Cha me nar do much, we a play some dominoes, some football, some sounds.

GAIL: You have a team?

ZIPPY: Nar, over dey.

GAIL: Yes. What else?

ZIPPY: Fool around, talk.

GAIL: Ah, what do you talk about?

ZIPPY: All kinda ting, Rastafarian tings, an Ethiopia.

GAIL: Would you all like to go to Africa?

ZIPPY: Sure all a we want go dey some day.

GAIL: Good, well maybe we could go on a trip to see some exhibits from Africa.

ZIPPY: Where?

GAIL: In London, there's always something going on concerning Africa, you'd be surprised.

ZIPPY: But dat not Africa, dat a white man ting, dem a hypocrite, dem not genuine Africa, is Africa we want ter see, we want ter see real lion not dem circus ting.

GAIL: I see, but it would give you some idea, of what life is really like in Africa.

ZIPPY: Cha, but not Africa, we want ter know we in Africa dats what we want ter know, you a see.

GAIL: Yes, where are you from?

ZIPPY: Me from Jamaica.

GAIL: You were born in Jamaica?

ZIPPY: No, we born in London, but me people from Jamaica.

GAIL: But you speak with a Jamaican . . .

ZIPPY: Cha, me could talk London if me wanted to but me is a Rastafarian so me talk Ja.

GAIL: I see.

ZIPPY: Yer all genuine Rasta man him a talk Jamaican or else him not genuine.

GAIL: Yes, and all the other boys they were born in London?

ZIPPY: Some a dem born in Jamaica some born in London me do' know.

GAIL: Are they allowed to be upstairs so long?

ZIPPY: Cha Sandy she a cool, she left Marcus in charge. Him upstairs. You a want to see him we call im fer you.

GAIL: No. (*She gets up.*) I'll just look around. (*She looks at a poster.*)

ZIPPY: Dat is de Emperor Haile Selassie.

GAIL: Yes.

ZIPPY: You know him face?

GAIL: Yes.

ZIPPY: Cha, you is Rastafarian.

GAIL: Are women allowed to be Rastafarian?

ZIPPY: Cha yes man all black people is Rastafarian. Is what dem believe.

GAIL: I see you have a bar.

ZIPPY: Yes.

GAIL: Do you run it yourselves?

ZIPPY: Nar Sandy, it a only keep coke.

GAIL: Would you like to run it yourselves?

ZIPPY: Cha what for, it en make no profit, it fer someting ter drink, it do' need no running.

West Side Story
By Arthur Laurents and Stephen Sondheim

Anita, 20s; Maria, late teens; Tony, late teens

Like *Valentin and Valentina* (p.119), *West Side Story* is a modern-day variation on the *Romeo and Juliet* theme, only this time the setting is the West Side streets of New York City and the form is a musical play (lyrics by Stephen Sondheim with music by Leonard Bernstein). Once again love is the central theme as two young people confront their families' cultural prejudices and the pressures of their street-wise peers in the hope of living happily together.

In Scene 7, Maria and her friend Anita are finishing work for the day, when Tony, Maria's boyfriend, arrives.

Maria, in a smock, is hand-sewing a wedding veil as Anita whirls in whipping off her smock.

ANITA: She's gone! That old bag of a *bruja* has gone!

MARIA: *Bravo!*

ANITA: The day is over, the jail is open, home we go!

MARIA: You go, *querida.* I will lock up.

ANITA: Finish tomorrow. Come!

MARIA: But I am in no hurry.

ANITA: I am. I'm going to take a bubble bath all during supper: Black Orchid.

MARIA: You will not eat?

ANITA: After the rumble – with 'Nardo.

MARIA: (*Sewing, angrily.*) That rumble, why do they have to do it?

ANITA: You saw how they dance: like they have to get rid of something, quick. That's how they fight.

MARIA: To get rid of what?

ANITA: Too much feeling. And they get rid of it: after a fight, that brother of yours is so healthy! Definitely: Black Orchid.
    (*There is a knock at rear door, and Tony enters.*)

TONY: *Buenas noches!*

ANITA: (*Sarcastically, to Maria.*) "You go, *querida.* I will lock up."
   (*To Tony.*) It's too early for *noches. Buenas tardes.*
TONY: (*Bows.*) *Gracias. Buenas tardes.*
MARIA: He just came to deliver aspirin.
ANITA: You'll need it.
TONY: No, we're out of the world.
ANITA: You're out of your heads.
TONY: We're twelve feet in the air.
MARIA: (*Gently taking his hand.*) Anita can see all that. (*To Anita.*)
   You will not tell?
ANITA: Tell what? How can I hear what goes on twelve feet over
   my head? (*Opens door. To Maria.*) You better be home in
   fifteen minutes. (*She goes out.*)
TONY: Don't worry. She likes us!
MARIA: But she is worried.
TONY: She's foolish. We're untouchable; we *are* in the air; we have
   magic!
MARIA: Magic is also evil and black. Are you going to that rumble?
TONY: No.
MARIA: Yes.
TONY: Why??
MARIA: You must go and stop it.
TONY: I have stopped it! It's only a fist fight. 'Nardo won't get –
MARIA: *Any* fight is not good for us.
TONY: Everything is good for us and we are good for everything.
MARIA: Listen and *hear* me. You must go and stop it.
TONY: Then I will.
MARIA: (*Surprised.*) Can you?
TONY: You don't even want a fist fight? There won't be any fight.
MARIA: I believe you! You *do* have magic.
TONY: Of course, I have you. You go home and dress up. Then
   tonight, I will come by for you.
MARIA: You cannot come by. My mama . . .
TONY: (*After a pause.*) Then I will take you to my house –
MARIA: (*Shaking her head.*) Your mama . . .
   (*Another awkward pause. Then he sees a female dummy and*

pushes it forward.)

TONY: She will come running from the kitchen to welcome you. She lives in the kitchen.

MARIA: Dressed so elegant?

TONY: I told her you were coming. She will look at your face and try not to smile. And she will say: Skinny – but pretty.

MARIA: She is plump, no doubt.

TONY: (*Holding out the waist of dummy's dress.*) Fat!

MARIA: (*Indicating another female dummy.*) I take after my mama; delicate-boned. (*He kisses her.*) Not in front of Mama! (*He turns the dummy around as she goes to a male dummy.*) Oh, I would like to see Papa in this! Mama will make him ask about your prospects, if you go to church. But Papa – Papa *might* like you.

TONY: (*Kneeling to the "father" dummy.*) May I have your daughter's hand?

MARIA: He says yes.

TONY: *Gracias!*

MARIA: And your mama?

TONY: I'm afraid to ask her.

MARIA: Tell her she's not getting a daughter; she's getting rid of a son.

TONY: She says yes.

MARIA: She has good taste. (*She grabs up the wedding veil and puts it on as Tony arranges the dummies.*)

TONY: Maid of honor!

MARIA: That color is bad for Anita.

TONY: Best man!

MARIA: That is my Papa!

TONY: Sorry, Papa. Here we go, Riff: Womb to Tomb! (*He takes hat off dummy.*)

MARIA: Now you see, Anita, I told you there was nothing to worry about.

SCENES
FOR
TWO WOMEN

A Shayna Maidel
By Barbara Lebow

Hanna and Lusia, range from 14 to late 20s

Set in 1946 *A Shayna Maidel* focuses on the recently reunited Weiss family. Although
Rose and her father escaped the horrors of Nazi Germany, her mother, who remained in
Poland to care for Rose's ailing sister, Lusia, perished in a concentration camp. Lusia
survived, and has now made her way to New York to be reunited with her family. The
play moves back and forth in time, recreating much of the troubled past through
theatrical dream sequences in which the characters are younger.

The first scene is set in Chernov, Poland, 1932, a memory from Lusia's past. In this
memory, Lusia and her childhood friend, Hanna, are about fourteen years old. Lusia has
come from the kitchen, having stolen a piece of honey cake for herself and Hanna. Alone
with Hanna, Lusia speaks of her affection for her mother.

HANNA: I love your mother. (*Lusia nods.*) Only I wish she wasn't so
sad. Even when she's joking, like now, I can see she's sad
underneath.
LUSIA: (*Shrugging.*) She misses my sister. And Papa, I think. But
mostly my sister.
HANNA: It seems like such a long time to be missing anyone.
LUSIA: Four years is nothing, Mama says. A child is a part of your
body you never stop missing. Sometimes she goes like this . . .
(*Quick intake of breath, hand to solar plexus.*) and she says,
"Rayzel is sick, I can feel it," or "Rayzel is frightened. She's
crying for her mama." It's the same as when someone's foot
gets cut off and it still itches.
HANNA: What about you? Do you still miss them?
LUSIA: Rayzel, maybe. A little bit. I used to very much. I missed her
and I was even jealous. Rayzel and Papa going to America and
I was sick with scarlet fever. My hair all fell out. I looked
terrible. I always thought we'd be going soon, too, and we still
might, any day now, but then I'd miss you and I know you
better than my sister. (*They lean across the table, close*

together, holding hands.) She's just a baby, anyway. Eight years old. So everything is good the way it is.

HANNA: (*An admission.*) I'm glad you got scarlet fever.

LUSIA: I'll tell you a secret, Hanna . . . Me. too. (*Looks toward kitchen before she goes on.*) You must swear never to tell this to anyone, ever . . . (*Hanna nods. They take an apparently oft-used swearing position.*) I'm glad I have Mama all to myself! When I was little and scared in the night she wouldn't let me in, with Papa there and the baby crying. But then, when they left, she would open the covers like a great wing and pull me close to her. She's different without Papa here. She sings. And she never made jokes when he was around. I don't remember her laughing out loud. Papa used to make us be quiet. He would get angry all of a sudden and you never knew when. (*Hanna and Lusia continue glancing toward the kitchen through the following dialogue.*)

HANNA: Do you suppose she loves him?

LUSIA: I don't know. It's hard to think of your mother that way. I think she does, from far away. Maybe more, from far away. You know, my father's a whole lot older than she is.

HANNA: He is?

LUSIA: Around fifty-something.

HANNA: I think that's very romantic.

LUSIA: I don't.

HANNA: To have someone like that to take care of you, who knows more than you do. With silver-gray in his hair. My parents aren't romantic at all.

LUSIA: Your parents are just short. They don't look romantic, that's all. It's not their fault.

HANNA: But they never talk, except about business, and they sleep in two different beds.

LUSIA: They do? (*Hanna nods.*) Mine used to have one. I thought everyone's parents did.

HANNA: I will.

LUSIA: Me, too.

HANNA: With Duvid Pechenik?

LUSIA: Shhh!

HANNA: He called you "dumpling."

LUSIA: That means he likes me.

HANNA: But he's just your age.

LUSIA: A year older!

HANNA: He has pimples.

LUSIA: So do you.

HANNA: Stop it! (*The girls' voices are getting louder. They stand up.*)

LUSIA: You stop it!

HANNA: Dumpling!

LUSIA: Midget parents!

[MAMA: (*Calling from offstage.*) What's going on in there?]

HANNA and LUSIA: Nothing.

[MAMA: (*Enters from the kitchen.*) You know, one old friend is worth ten new ones.]

LUSIA: I know, Mama, but if she just wasn't so picky.

[MAMA: If your grandma had a beard, she'd be your grandpa.]

HANNA: We understand.

(*Lusia and Hanna smile, giggle, and shake their heads.*)

Hanna and Lusia, range from 14 to late 20s

In the second scene, Rose's apartment in new York City, 1946, Lusia's memory of her childhood friend, Hanna, mixes the past and the present.

Tuesday afternoon. When lights rise, Lusia is in the living room, energetically cleaning with a brush and cloth. She is humming, on her knees. The lights shift to a glow. Facing Downstage, she smiles as Hanna enters behind her.

LUSIA: Hanna.

HANNA: *Ken ich arayn kumen?*

LUSIA: (*Running to embrace her.*) Hanna! *Ch'ob gevart far dir!* (*Hanna now looks Lusia's age and is dressed in outdated, secondhand clothes like hers.*)

HANNA: But your sister isn't home. Are you sure it's all right?

LUSIA: (*Leading Hanna by the hand. When she speaks, it is reminiscent of the first time Rose showed her the apartment.*) If she were here, she'd invite you in herself. You have to see everything. It's even got things we didn't know to dream about! Look here, look at this: carpet like a cloud. You could sleep on the floor. And what about this? This is a machine that makes it warm, like the middle of July, on the coldest winter day! (*Hanna exclaims over everything.*) And, Hanna, wait till you see the kitchen!

HANNA: Does it have a stove? A real one?

LUSIA: It runs on electricity, that's what you won't believe. (*Lusia runs into the kitchen.*)

HANNA: (*Looking after her.*) No!

LUSIA: (*Offstage.*) Yes! I mean it! And there's a machine that washes your clothes and then the dishes. Oh, it leaves a little egg sometimes, that you have to do over. But mostly it's like having a housemaid – five maids – to do the work. (*Lusia comes back into the dinette.*) And you put your garbage outside the back door and while you sleep, a man comes on an elevator and takes it away.

HANNA: There's something left to throw away?

LUSIA: Too much. You can't eat enough to use it up before it spoils.

HANNA: We used to dream of a piece of bread (*She rubs the table top.*) Everything is so clean!

LUSIA: (*Back in the living room, turns to Hanna.*) Wait until you see the bathroom! Everything white and shiny. A bathtub big enough to swim in and water hot enough to boil an egg if you wanted to.

HANNA: Inside the house? (*Lusia nods. They laugh.*) And I can stay here?

LUSIA: Of course. Rose is out of town on business. You can have the bedroom – I'll show it to you in a minute – and I'll sleep here. It's where I'm used to. (*She poses on the sofa like Rose. They look at each other, then Lusia sits up and speaks softly.*)

You know that whatever is mine is yours, Hanna.

HANNA: (*Arms held out to Lusia, who joins her.*) Whatever is mine is yours.

LUSIA: A half a potato.

HANNA: A quarter of a potato . . . A cup of barley-water soup.

LUSIA: A spoonful of soup. Half is yours.

HANNA: More than half sometimes.

LUSIA: Whoever needs it more.

HANNA: Whoever wants it less.

(*Pause. The lights are beginning a slow change to cold blue.*)

LUSIA: You kept me alive.

HANNA: Your life was something to live for.

LUSIA: You were all I had left.

HANNA: You were everything.

(*Pause. Their bodies are beginning to change, distort. They are clutching, rather than holding each other.*)

LUSIA: If you had no one you were dead . . .

HANNA: . . . . much faster. If you had someone . . .

LUSIA: . . . you had to live so they would live.

(*It is cold. A distant wind is blowing. Hanna and Lusia reach around each other even further, leaning on one another for physical support and warmth. Hanna breaks away, looks around.*)

HANNA: (*Whispering.*) Now follow me. Into the house.

(*Hanna moves toward the bedroom. Lusia pulls back, frightened.*)

LUSIA: But we can't go in there.

(*Both women are weak and cold. Hanna has the energy given by a fever.*)

HANNA: Yes we can!

LUSIA: No!

HANNA: But we're free!

LUSIA: I don't believe it.

HANNA: Liberated.

LUSIA: Liberated.

HANNA: He said it was all right. The Russian on his horse. He said the whole town belongs to us now.

LUSIA: (*Close to Hanna, outside the bedroom, whispering, terrified.*) But there might be someone in there.

HANNA: So what? Old women and babies only. They were left behind.

LUSIA: I wouldn't put my foot in a German house.

HANNA: It was a Polish house before they took it.

LUSIA: It's no good, Hanna. It had Nazis in it.

HANNA: We're free. We can go where we want to. We can take anything. Food. Clothes. Take back what they stole. He told us. The Russian on his horse. In Yiddish. Who would have guessed? In Yiddish.

LUSIA: But there's a grandmother in there, Hanna. And a little baby. We might frighten them.

HANNA: How can you say such a thing? Your mother wasn't frightened? (*As Hanna speaks, Lusia covers her ears, humming, to drown her out.*) Sprinze wasn't frightened on the way to the ovens? They took your sweet little girl. They took your mother. They took everything from us, but we can't take a warm coat or a piece of sausage from –

LUSIA: Stop! I don't want to hear! We can't be like them! We can't do what they did! And I don't want a warm coat. I want to be cold like the dead ones. I don't want –

HANNA: Shhh! See. She ran away. (*Leading Lusia into the bedroom. The wind stops.*) Took the baby out the window. Look. Lusia. It's empty. Come. There's nobody here. Look. A bowl of cereal. For the baby. Oatmeal. Still hot. And a sausage. Milk.

LUSIA: It will make you sick to eat all at once. Just take a little bit, Hanna!

(*But Hanna is eating the imaginary food rapidly, insanely. Then she sees the doll. She picks it up and cradles it like a baby.*)

HANNA: This is for my baby.

LUSIA: It belongs to another child.

HANNA: It's for the future. For my baby.

LUSIA: You'd bring a child into this world? Anyway, we can't have children anymore.

HANNA: I can.

LUSIA: You can't, Hanna. I can't. We stopped our periods. We're not women anymore. We don't have women's bodies.

HANNA: We will. (*Lusia turns away from her.*) Eat. And get round. Soft. Clean. Bleed. (*She is weakening, having difficulty breathing, crumples on the bed. Lusia turns to her.*) Have babies. You and Duvid.

LUSIA: (*Moving to comfort Hanna.*) All right, Hanna. We'll have babies.

HANNA: (*Hugging the doll tightly.*) And me . . .

LUSIA: You with someone wonderful like Duvid.

HANNA: A handsome Russian soldier.

LUSIA: On a horse.

HANNA: Who, out of nowhere, speaks Yiddish.

LUSIA: (*Laughing.*) The horse?

HANNA: Even the horse speaks Yiddish.

(*Hanna and Lusia both start laughing wildly until Hanna begins to cough. She weakens greatly.*)

LUSIA: Shh. Soon you'll be better. Now there'll be doctors and medicine.

HANNA: (*Giving Lusia the doll.*) I ate too much. You were right. But it's a good reason to be sick for a change. Overeating. What would mama say? (*She rises with effort.*) Here, you take the doll.

LUSIA: But it's yours.

HANNA: You'll need it before I do. Don't even know the Russian's name yet. Let go of me. (*She pushes Lusia away.*) Hold the doll. Protect it. I'm going to throw up and I don't want to get it dirty. (*Lusia stands up as Hanna exits.*) Not dirty. Go away from me, Lusia. *Gai avek fun mir. Avek!* (*Lusia is standing alone, hugging the doll, as the lights return to normal. She looks at the doll, caresses it.*)

LUSIA: Hannele! Who can I laugh with now?

And The Soul Shall Dance
By Wakako Yamauchi

Masako, 12; Kiyoko, 14

The action of Wakako Yamauchi's *And The Soul Shall Dance* takes place on and between two small farms in Southern California's Imperial Valley in the early 1930s. Old world Japan and the promise of fortune in the new world of America form the spine of this stirring story of two Japanese families struggling for a better life. Murata, one of the two farmers, echoes the desire of the Japanese immigrants when he says, "That's everyone's dream. Make money, go home and live like a king." The promise that brought them all to the United States is fading as the disappointment of the daily struggle to survive grows. The complication deepens when Oka, the other farmer, brings his daughter to America, after years of saving to have her join them. As the two couples argue and debate the virtues of living in the United States, Murata's daughter, Masako, and Oka's newly arrived daughter, Kiyoko, establish a relationship – one that plays host to similar cultural discussions but also addresses the quest for growing into adults and making their own decisions about their lives.

In this scene, Masako and Kiyoko engage in a small battle of culture and language.

The Murata house and yard. Hana and Murata have already left the house to examine the rain damage in the fields. Masako prepares to go to school. She puts on a coat and picks up her books and lunch bag. Meanwhile, Kiyoko slips quietly into the yard. She wears a coat and carries Murata's robe. She sets it on the outside bench. Masako walks out and is surprised to see Kiyoko.

MASAKO: Hi. I thought you'd be . . . sick today.

KIYOKO: Oh. I woke up late.

MASAKO: (*Scrutinizing Kiyoko's face.*) Your eyes are red.

KIYOKO: (*Averting her eyes.*) Oh. I . . . got . . . sand in it. Yes.

MASAKO: Do you want to use eye drops? We have eye drops in the house.

KIYOKO: Oh . . . no. That's all right.

MASAKO: That's what you call bloodshot.

KIYOKO: Oh.

MASAKO: My father gets it a lot. When he drinks too much.

KIYOKO: Oh . . .

MASAKO: (*Notices Kiyoko doesn't have her lunch.*) Where's your lunch bag?

KIYOKO: I . . . forgot it.

MASAKO: Did you make your lunch today?

KIYOKO: Yes. Yes, I did. But I forgot it.

MASAKO: Do you want to go back and get it?

KIYOKO: No, that's all right. (*They are silent for a while.*) We'll be late.

MASAKO: Do you want to practice your words?

KIYOKO: (*Thoughtfully.*) Oh . . .

MASAKO: Say, "My."

KIYOKO: My?

MASAKO: Eyes . . .

KIYOKO: Eyes.

MASAKO: Are . . .

KIYOKO: Are.

MASAKO: Red.

KIYOKO: Red.

MASAKO: Your eyes are red. (*Kiyoko doesn't repeat it.*) I . . . (*Kiyoko doesn't cooperate.*) Say, "I."

KIYOKO: I.

MASAKO: Got . . .

KIYOKO: Got.

MASAKO: Sand . . . (*Kiyoko balks.*) Say, "I."

KIYOKO: (*Sighing.*) I.

MASAKO: Reft . . .

KIYOKO: Reft.

MASAKO: My . . .

KIYOKO: My.

MASAKO: Runch . . .

KIYOKO: Run . . . lunch. (*She stops.*) Masako-san, you are mean. You are hurting me.

MASAKO: It's a joke! I was just trying to make you laugh!

KIYOKO: I cannot laugh today.

MASAKO: Sure you can. You can laugh. Laugh! Like this. (*She makes a hearty laugh.*)

KIYOKO: I cannot laugh when you make fun of me.

MASAKO: Okay, I'm sorry. We'll practice some other words then, okay? (*Kiyoko doesn't answer.*) Say, "Okay."

KIYOKO: (*Reluctantly.*) Okay . . .

MASAKO: Okay, then . . . um . . . um . . . (*She still teases and talks rapidly.*) Say . . . um . . . "She sells sea shells on the seashore." (*Kiyoko turns away indignantly.*) Aw, come on, Kiyoko! It's just a joke. Laugh!

KIYOKO: (*Imitating sarcastically.*) Ha-ha-ha! Now you say, "*Kono kyaku wa yoku kaki ku kyaku da* [This guest eats a lot of persimmons]*!*"

MASAKO: Sure! I can say it! *Kono kyaku waki ku kyoku kaku . . .*

KIYOKO: That's not right.

MASAKO: *Koki kuki kya . . .*

KIYOKO: No.

MASAKO: Okay, then. You say, "Sea sells she shells . . . shu . . . sss . . ." (*They both laugh, Kiyoko with her hands over her mouth. Masako takes Kiyoko's hands from her mouth.*) Not like that! Like this! (*She gives a big belly laugh.*)

KIYOKO: Like this? (*She imitates Masako.*)

MASAKO: Yeah, that's right! You're not mad anymore?

KIYOKO: I'm not mad anymore.

MASAKO: Okay. You can share my lunch today because we're . . .

KIYOKO: "Flends?"

Family Scenes
By Ivette M. Ramirez

Paula, 23; Sophia, 20

Family Scenes depicts the fragile life of a contemporary Hispanic family in which the mother, Margarita, attempts to protect her daughters, Paula and Sophia, from the truth by presenting herself as the typical wife who has been abandoned by her husband. When the daughters discover that the mother's innocent deceptions are only escapism and have little to do with meeting the challenges of daily life, we learn, as Sophia says, "The lies hurt more than the truth." Strong family relationships can only be built through shared experiences.

In this scene, the rather hot-tempered Sophia is waiting up for her more even-tempered sister, Paula.

The stage is dark except for a light on the bedroom and a very dim light coming from the living room. Sophia is watching television while in bed. Paula comes up the stairs to the brownstone, then quietly into the apartment and tiptoes into the bedroom.

PAULA: What are you doing up?

SOPHIA: Mommie was piss furious when she went to bed.

PAULA: It isn't that late.

SOPHIA: Tell that to her. You have a good time?

PAULA: (*Getting undressed.*) Shut up and leave me alone.

SOPHIA: What I do? Just 'cause I wasn't Miss Sweet with that jerk.

PAULA: Don't call him a jerk.

SOPHIA: I can't help it if he's a low life.

PAULA: What's with you?

SOPHIA: He's just using you and you know it.

PAULA: You don't know what you're talking about. Benny loves me.

SOPHIA: Sure, he does.

PAULA: What's with you, anyway. Benny and I have been going out for six months, why are you acting so obnoxious now?

SOPHIA: You know that wedding of yours is going to upset everyone.

PAULA: What are you talking about?

SOPHIA: You asked Dad to come to the wedding. Do you really think Mom wants to see him after all these years? Do you? Why do you have to have him at your wedding?

PAULA: None of this is any of your business, so stay out of it.

SOPHIA: Why do you want to hurt Mom that way?

PAULA: I'm not hurting Mom, or anything, I just want my wedding to be proper. He is my father and he should give me away.

SOPHIA: How come you act so ancient. He's nothing to us, when we needed him where was he? When we were on welfare?

PAULA: You don't know anything. That was a long time ago. You don't know what happened between them, we had nothing to do with it.

SOPHIA: Well, where has he been all these years? He's in Chicago living this wonderful, carefree life, no responsibility. He never sent us a dime.

PAULA: That's not true.

SOPHIA: Oh, excuse me, a few miserable dollars every few years, maybe a gift at Christmas. I'm sorry I can't forgive him for what he did.

PAULA: Who's asking you to do anything. It's my wedding and this is what I want, a proper wedding. Now, if that bothers you, tough.

SOPHIA: It's going to be tough on you 'cause he doesn't give a shit about us or this wedding. He ain't going to come.

PAULA: You mean he doesn't care about me. He's always loved you best.

SOPHIA: You're wrong, he doesn't care about either of us or Mom.

PAULA: (*Finding the picture in the drawer.*) Sure, that's why the first person he asks me for is you when I call him. Why do you hate him so much? (*Paula places the picture back on the dresser and gets into bed.*)

SOPHIA: I just don't like fairy tales. I don't believe in them.

PAULA: Sure, you don't have to. If you were getting married, Dad

would be here like a shot. But I made sure he'd answer my
letter this time.

SOPHIA: What you do?

PAULA: I told him you were looking forward towards the wedding
and wanted to see him again.

SOPHIA: How could you do that?

PAULA: I'm sure I'll get a letter from him soon.

SOPHIA: I don't want to hear it anymore, he ain't anything to me.
(*Sophia buries her head in her pillow.*)

PAULA: (*Turning off the light.*) You're such a bitch.

SOPHIA: Yeah, but a smart bitch.
(*The light in the living room goes off leaving the stage dark.*)

For Julia
By Margareta Garpe; Translated by Harry G. Carlson

Gloria, 40s; Julia, 18

In *For Julia*, Margareta Garpe, one of Sweden's leading contemporary dramatists, explores the relationship between mothers and daughters and the unique place young people hold in our modern world.

The scene below introduces Julia's relationship with her mother, Gloria.

Gloria enters from the bathroom, dressed in a bathrobe and wiping the last of the mask from her face with a towel. She takes a cigarette out of her handbag but finds that her lighter won't work. She hunts for matches.

GLORIA: It's Strindberg's *Miss Julie.*

JULIA: Which part . . . ?

GLORIA: (*Sarcastically.*) The butler . . . (*Frustrated over not finding matches.*) Dammit!

JULIA: (*Crossing to the bookcase.*) No matches here either . . . I know I didn't throw *Pippi* away. Did you?

GLORIA: . . . or Kristine, the cook. What did you think it would be?

JULIA: Miss Julie . . .

GLORIA: Then why did you ask? You know damned well I want to play Julie.

JULIA: Sorry. (*Gloria finds a matchbox, shakes it, and opens it.*)

GLORIA: Why do I save used matches? (*She continues searching in Julia's room.*)

JULIA: I don't smoke!

GLORIA: Unbelievable. Not a match in the whole house! (*With rising panic.*) I can't very well go out like this and buy some . . . (*She lifts up the telephone receiver and checks to make sure she hears a dial tone. Julia rises, hops up on a chair, and finds a box of matches resting on the top of a picture frame. She waves it triumphantly.*)

JULIA: Your old hiding place . . .

GLORIA: Fantastic . . . I'll never forget the morning . . .

JULIA: As a kid I couldn't reach this high.

GLORIA: . . . I woke up smelling something strange . . . Smoke . . .
(*Looking in the matchbox.*) Two left. (*She lights a cigarette.
Julia hands her a candle, which she lights.*) I leaped out of bed
and found you sitting on the sofa. You were only three but
you'd made sandwiches and something approaching coffee . . .
And you'd put candles in the candlesticks and lit them. It
looked like high mass on Christmas Eve. And you sat there so
devoutly, staring at the candles. By the time I got up they had
almost burned down. A couple of them were flickering close
to the curtains . . . They're all still there. All the memories. Like
rolls of undeveloped film. All of a sudden a picture plops
down in the developer . . .

JULIA: I just remembered you used to keep them up there . . .
(*Gloria inspects her face in the mirror. Julia continues to
inspect books. She collects a pile of Heidi books, which she
throws away, one after the other.*)

GLORIA: That was a welcome memory. Then there are other pictures
that should be left to yellow in some locked drawer . . . But
even if you lock up the copies, the negatives remain . . .
(*Gloria is suddenly conscious of what Julia is doing.*) Julia! You
can't throw those away!

JULIA: Why, do you want them?

GLORIA: They were gifts. From your grandmother.

JULIA: But I read them. And Grandma's dead . . . Or maybe you
think she's sitting up there now, looking down on us?
Watching little Julia throw out all her old birthday presents.

GLORIA: (*After a pause.*) No. I don't believe that . . .

JULIA: How do you know?

GLORIA: Because the dead are dead. Stone cold dead.

JULIA: How do you know the dead don't go on living?

GLORIA: They're only immortal as long as we remember them. They
can haunt us only as long as we let them . . . You're right.
Throw them away . . . Now that I think about it, I threw mine

away too. With a feeling of guilt, I guess. For Grandma who was dead and would grieve to see Gloria throw away the presents she paid for out of her meager pocketbook. And for the starving children of Africa . . . Think how happy they'd be to get fourteen volumes of Heidi in Swedish . . .
(*Julia, browsing through her books, opens one.*)

JULIA: (*Reads.*) "To Julia, on her tenth birthday, from grandmother." This was the last one. And she didn't even give it to me herself. It was just sitting there on the table, beautifully wrapped. With a cake that had ten burned-down candles. I'd been lying in bed waiting for congratulations. Finally, I got up to get ready for school. You were sitting alone on the sofa, with your coat on. Staring at the candles. "Grandma died last night," you said. You were so calm. Not a tear. "Grandma wanted to die," you said. And you gave me this book from her. And neither of us cried? Wasn't that strange? (*Julia tosses all but the last of the books in a black trash bag.*)

GLORIA: She couldn't stand solitude, but she couldn't break out of it.

JULIA: But if she bought me a present, she must have planned to bring it herself, as usual . . .

GLORIA: (*Evasively.*) Unhappy people don't act logically.

JULIA: Oh, I know that – only too well. (*Pause.*) I'm just going to pack up my things quickly. I'm only taking what I really need. (*Julia puts her grandmother's present in the carton. Gloria waves her hands aimlessly, trying to get her nail polish to dry.*)

GLORIA: Do you have to leave tonight . . . ? Why tonight? What's the hurry? Henrik was going to drive your things . . .

JULIA: I got the key and I don't want to take a chance . . .

GLORIA: I'm not trying to stand in your way.

JULIA: . . . that the landlord will change his mind and say I can't live in Emma's apartment . . .

GLORIA: I haven't even seen it. You're moving someplace I haven't even seen . . .

JULIA: You'll have to come and visit. I'll invite you to dinner . . .

(*Gloria takes the bouquet out of the vase.*)

GLORIA: So it's going to be "So long, Gloria. Thanks for everything. Take care . . . " (*She tears the paper off the bouquet.*) Daisies and cornflowers . . . daisies and cornflowers . . . Just like Midsummer Eve. You were five, and we were picking flowers to make garlands. Up in the house they were getting ready for the big party. And we were waiting. Your dress was still spotless . . . I braided two garlands.

JULIA: Three . . . You always forget Charlie . . .

GLORIA: . . . and I thought . . . freeze this moment. Let her remember it. Julia and Gloria together on a meadow on Midsummer Eve . . .

(*Julia grabs the bouquet brusquely from Gloria and carefully rewraps it.*)

JULIA: These are to Emma from Gustav.

GLORIA: I even ironed your dress. (*Pause.*) Gustav? Isn't he dead?

JULIA: You should see Emma when she gets flowers . . .

GLORIA: How the hell can Gustav send flowers to Emma when he's dead?

JULIA: She blushes . . . and smells every flower . . .

GLORIA: Julia!

JULIA: You just don't want me to move away from home.

GLORIA: Crap!

JULIA: We all take turns buying flowers for Emma, from Gustav.

GLORIA: You're letting poor Emma live a lie. Just to get her apartment.

JULIA: I'm keeping a human being alive . . . and getting my own life . . .

GLORIA: And you haven't had one here . . . ?

JULIA: Yeah . . .

GLORIA: Have I stood in your way?

JULIA: . . . no . . .

GLORIA: What are you *really* saying?

JULIA: Just what I said . . . that you never stood in my way . . .

GLORIA: You don't sound especially convincing . . . (*She crosses to Julia, who pulls away and goes out into the hall.*)

The House of Bernarda Alba
By Federíco García Lorca;
Translated by James Graham-Lujan and Richard L. O'Connell

Adela, early twenties; Martirio, late twenties

Set in rural Castile, Spain, this dark tragedy opens just after the death of Bernarda Alba's second husband. Bernarda, who rules her house and her five daughters with an iron hand, declares that the family will go into secluded mourning for eight years. She suppresses all emotion and forbids her daughters to associate with the young men of the village. The eldest daughter is already engaged to be married to Pepe, one of the villagers, but, when the third daughter, Martirio, who also loves the man, discovers that her youngest sister, Adela, has been paying visits to the young man, she tells Bernarda. Bernarda attempts to shoot Pepe but fails; however, she tells Adela that she has killed him. Upon hearing this news, Adela hangs herself. Bernarda, unyielding to the end, proclaims that her daughter died a virgin.

In this scene, Martirio admonishes Adela to stay away from Pepe.

MARTIRIO: (*In a low voice.*) Adela!
    (*Pause. She advances to the door. Then, calling,*) Adela!
    (*Adela enters. Her hair is disarranged.*)
ADELA: And what are you looking for me for?
MARTIRIO: Keep away from him.
ADELA: Who are you to tell me that?
MARTIRIO: That's no place for a decent woman.
ADELA: How you wish *you'd* been there!
MARTIRIO: (*Shouting.*) This is the moment for me to speak. This can't go on.
ADELA: This is just the beginning. I've had strength enough to push myself forward – the spirit and looks you lack. I've seen death under this roof, and gone out to look for what was mine, what belonged to me.
MARTIRIO: That soulless man came for another woman. You pushed yourself in front of him.
ADELA: He came for the money, but his eyes were always on me.

MARTIRIO: I won't allow you to snatch him away. He'll marry Angustias.

ADELA: You know better than I he doesn't love her.

MARTIRIO: I know.

ADELA: You know because you've seen – he loves me, me!

MARTIRIO: (*Desperately.*) Yes.

ADELA: (*Close before her.*) He loves me, *me!* He loves me, *me!*

MARTIRIO: Stick me with a knife if you like, but don't tell me that again.

ADELA: That's why you're trying to fix it so I won't go away with him. It makes no difference to you if he puts his arms around a woman he doesn't love. Nor does it to me. He could be a hundred years with Angustias, but for him to have his arms around me seems terrible to you – because you too love him! You love him!

MARTIRIO: (*Dramatically.*) Yes! Let me say it without hiding my head. Yes! My breast's bitter, bursting like a pomegranate. I love him!

ADELA: (*Impulsively, hugging her.*) Martirio, Martirio, I'm not to blame!

MARTIRIO: Don't put your arms around me! Don't try to smooth it over. My blood's no longer yours, and even though I try to think of you as a sister, I see you as just another woman. (*She pushes her away.*)

ADELA: There's no way out here. Whoever has to drown – let her drown. Pepe is mine. He'll carry me to the rushes along the river bank . . .

MARTIRIO: He won't!

ADELA: I can't stand this horrible house after the taste of his mouth. I'll be what he wants me to be. Everybody in the village against me, burning me with fiery fingers; pursued by those who claim they're decent, and I'll wear, before them all, the crown of thorns that belongs to the mistress of a married man.

MARTIRIO: Hush!

ADELA: Yes, yes. (*In a low voice.*) Let's go to bed. Let's let him marry Angustias. I don't care any more, but I'll go off alone to a little house where he'll come to see me whenever he wants, whenever he feels like it.

MARTIRIO: That'll never happen! Not while I have a drop of blood left in my body.

ADELA: Not just weak you, but a wild horse I could force to his knees with just the strength of my little finger.

MARTIRIO: Don't raise that voice of yours to me. It irritates me. I have a heart full of a force so evil that, without my wanting to be, I'm drowned by it.

ADELA: You show us the way to love our sisters. God must have meant to leave me alone in the midst of darkness, because I can see you as I've never seen you before.

(*A whistle is heard and Adela runs toward the door, but Martirio gets in front of her.*)

MARTIRIO: Where are you going?

ADELA: Get away from that door!

MARTIRIO: Get by me if you can!

ADELA: Get away!

(*They struggle.*)

MARTIRIO: (*Shouts.*) Mother! Mother!

ADELA: Let me go!

Redwood Curtain
By Lanford Wilson

Geri, 17; Geneva, mid-forties

Lanford Wilson's *Redwood Curtain* portrays the journey of a young Eurasian girl, the daughter of a Vietnamese woman and an American G.I., who has been adopted by wealthy Americans. Set in the Redwood forests of northern California, Geri searches for her natural father, whom she believes to be among the transient Vietnam veterans who have been taken refuge in the area.

In the first scene below, Geri speaks with her aunt, whom she is staying with, about the conflicting feelings she has as a young professional pianist.

◆ ◆ ◆ ◆

GERI: Why anyone would want to be involved, even peripherally, with music is beyond me. Nobody *ever* listens. We go to the opera, everyone, I mean *everyone,* is asleep. Music is Ovaltine to them. Mother had all these intellectual types over, all they talked about all weekend was this concert. Zubin Mehta was guest conductor on *Live from London* or something, they all know him, of course. They go in the TV room, they turn on the TV, they start with the "He's let his hair grow, he looks very distinguished, I love his tails . . . " and the architectural detail of Albert Hall, which they didn't like and you couldn't see anyway, and all the music they've heard there, and how foul the food was at the "interval," and all the music they've heard all over Europe and the food they had *there,* and finally just the *food* they've had. They didn't hear a note of music.
GENEVA: You should have taped it.
GERI: The point was to hear it live from London. Also, I don't know how to work the VCR. The one time I got it to tape anything, I set it to record *Cheers,* I came home, I'd taped an entire Yankee-Oakland game. The As literally cleaned New York's clock. Also, the program was "Mostly Mahler," which is not my idea of a fun evening.

GENEVA: You're sounding bitter.

GERI: You're darned right I'm bitter. I practice like a dog for twelve years, get exercised to tears over some nuance of theory for godsake over something nobody even hears. It's a rip-off. You know the average number of playing times for a CD? You don't, I read it last week – even pop records, the average number of times a record is played is one time and a quarter. And they want me to spend a week in some studio going over and over the *Goldberg Variations* like we need another recording of that? Forget it.

GENEVA: (*After a moment she lets that pass.*) Is that a good show, *Cheers?*

GERI: I love it, but I intend to marry Ted Danson. Do they really serve food during intermission at Albert Hall?

GENEVA: I imagine.

GERI: That is just so – typical. It's all Julia's friends talk about. During breakfast they talk about lunch; during lunch they start planning dinner. She had some winner of the National Book Award and this critic and a physicist and this Genius Painter and God knows how many really good musicians you might actually learn something from, sitting around the room arguing, and I mean almost to blows, over the best recipe for kreplach.

GENEVA: Which Mahler?

GERI: The Seventh. In E Minor, which is like insult to injury.

GENEVA: Is that why you're not practicing so much lately?

GERI: I'm not practicing at all. Ever again.

GENEVA: I can remember when you'd done a whole hour of scales by this time.

GERI: I thought I'd spare you.

GENEVA: You've always said you like this piano. Maybe we should trade. This one really belonged to your dad. Nobody ever plays it except you. If you like it better.

GERI: I don't want any of them. Leave it here.

GENEVA: My best memory of this room is bringing my breakfast in here at the crack of dawn and watching you play. Your dad conducting with a cigarette, counting out the time like a metronome.

GERI: A cigarette in one hand and a bottle of white wine in the other. You had to get to Laird before noon; his day was usually over about lunchtime.

GENEVA: I like scales and exercises. I always have. The sound of industry maybe.

GERI: (*She glares mildly at Geneva.*) You're really pushing it. Do you love the sawmill?

GENEVA: I loved the smell, not the noise.

GERI: If you really don't know I quit, I mean totally quit, then you're the only person in the nation that doesn't know, because Julia's been like broadcasting it. She doesn't really care but it's thrilling conversation. I'm going to Paris and – I don't know, study cooking. Learn to do something people understand.

◆ ◆ ◆ ◆

Geri, 17; Geneva, mid-forties

In the second scene, Geneva, Geri's aunt, joins Geri at a local coffee shop and tells her of a disturbing visit with the transient veteran Geri believes to be her father.

A coffeehouse in Arcata. Geri sits at a table with a cup of coffee, studying a map. After a moment, Geneva enters. She walks to the table and drops Geri's wallet on it.

GENEVA: Your putative father and Bitch dropped by the house. Get your stuff together and let's get out of here. This coffeehouse refuses to serve me. I sat here once for half an hour, nobody gave me the time of day.

GERI: They don't have table service, you have to go to the counter.

GENEVA: I'm too old to live in a college town.

GERI: What did he tell you?

GENEVA: He showed me his dog tags, probably the only identification he has. Right now, you've got that man so confused I don't think he knows if he's your father or not.

GERI: I think he is. What's his name?

GENEVA: If I told you it was nothing like Ray, would you still try to see him?

GERI: Are you crazy?

GENEVA: That's what I thought. (*She sits.*) He was obviously skulking around the house, waiting for you to leave. He showed up the moment you left. It was all I could do not to hit the panic button and call Julia. It took me a full hour to get myself together enough to try to find him.

GERI: Why?

GENEVA: You're not going to talk to that man again unless I'm there. I've driven up and down every street and alley in Arcata. Halfway to Ferndale, up 101 damn near to Larrupin'. I've put ninety miles on the car. I saw one of your swimming buddies in town.

GERI: I didn't go swimming.

GENEVA: I realize that. I asked the woman at the shelter if she'd seen John Doe, she said, "Oh, Geri was just asking about him." You didn't find him?

GERI: No. I think he's gone back to the woods.

GENEVA: Oh, God. I can't do it. I can't go back in there. (*Beat.*) His name is Lyman Fellers.

GERI: Lyman Fellers? I don't care. He has an eagle tattooed on his arm.

GENEVA: Ten thousand soldiers must have that tattoo. You told him about that, too?

GERI: No.

GENEVA: Well, it doesn't matter. I did. What is that, a map?

GERI: (*Showing Geneva the map.*) I think we were here. The closest place you could drive to is over here.

GENEVA: That's the other side of the fern valley. I can hardly tramp through the woods dressed liked this.

GERI: You know the way better than I do. It's not that far. If you go by the house you'll want to change clothes, then you'll want to leave a note for Barney. It'll be dark. I"m going. You can take me or not.

GENEVA: Geri, I'm exhausted. Is there sugar in that?

GERI: No.

(*Geneva puts sugar in the coffee, stirs it, and drinks it down.*)

GENEVA: Child, child, child. Why you want your father to be someone like that is . . .

GERI: I don't want it or not, I just think it's true. Don't you feel it? That kind of completely inhuman, asocial behavior. Wandering around by myself. Shut up in a two-by-four rehearsal room eight hours a day. Having so few friends. Not believing anything anyone says to me.

GENEVA: Well, whose fault is that?

GERI: Maybe it's his.

GENEVA: And no, I don't feel it. You're an artist. Artists are crazy.

GERI: No more.

GENEVA: Geri, he's not well. He's been – he's a – I'm trying to think of a way to talk about the man without sounding prejudicial or maudlin or – well, I can't.
But that's a fine reason to want to know your parents: having someone to blame your idiosyncrasies on. You actually followed him through the woods?

GERI: I thought maybe he'd, I don't know, *sing* to himself, or whistle or something.

GENEVA: Oh, God. If this doesn't kill me, Julia will kill me. Did he? Whistle?

GERI: He knew I was following him.

GENEVA: *I* whistle. I've even been known to sing to myself. Julia played the piano. David thinks he can play the guitar –

GERI: – Julia's never touched that piano in her life. It was Laird's piano.

GENEVA: You were brought up in a household that appreciates music. Some things are *learned*, Geri.

Shadow Of A Man
By Cherríe Moraga

Leticia, 17; Lupe, 12

Shadow Of A Man is set in the home of the Rodriguez's, a Mexican family living near Los Angeles; the time is 1969. At the heart of the family are the women: Hortensia, the mother; Rosario, the aunt, and the daughters, Lupe and Leticia. While Hortensia finds herself stifled by an abusive marriage, Aunt Rosario, who has remained unmarried, speaks up for what she believes is right. Young Leticia rebels against the old values and is seeking change for Chicana women. The men are but shadows in the lives of the women. The son, Rigo, is intent upon marrying a white girl, and the father, Manuel, upset with his son's decision and guilt ridden over past troubles, becomes distant, remote, and abusive. In the end, the women must find comfort in each other.

The scene below, between Leticia and Lupe, comes after the difficult night the family has learned that brother Rigo is going to marry a gringa.

Leticia and Lupe are in the bathroom, in their bathrobes. Leticia is standing in front of the mirror fixing her hair, while Lupe polishes a pair of white dress shoes. Manuel sits on the porch, drinking a beer, a six pack next to him. It is cloudy. Lucha Villa's "Que me lleva el tren" is playing on the radio.

LUPE: I liked Teresa better.

LETICIA: I liked Teresa, too, but Rigo thought he was too good for a Chicana, so he's going to marry a gringa.

LUPE: Well, he mus' love Karen.

LETICIA: Right.

LUPE: Doesn't he?

LETICIA: *(Referring to her hair.)* C'mere, Lupe. Help me.

LUPE: Well, does he?

LETICIA: Does he what?

LUPE: Love her. Does he love Karen?

LETICIA: Who knows what he feels, man. Jus' forget it. Do you hear me? Don't think about him no more. He's gone. In a couple of hours he'll be married and that's it. We'll never see him again.

(*Referring to her hairdo.*) Lupe, hand me the Dippity Do. (*Lupe gets up, gives her the styling gel. Leticia begins applying it to her bangs. Lupe moves in front of Leticia to face the mirror. She stretches open her eyelids with her fingers.*) Lupe, get out of the way.

LUPE: You can see yourself in there . . . in the darkest part.

LETICIA: What? (*Lupe leans into the mirror for a closer look.*)

LUPE: Two little faces, one in each eye. It's like you got other people living inside you. Maybe you're not really you. Maybe they're the real you and the big you is just a dream you.

LETICIA: I swear you give me the creeps when you talk about this stuff. You're gonna make yourself nuts.

LUPE: But I'm not kidding. I mean, how d'you know? How do you really know what's regular life and what's a sueño?

LETICIA: You're talking to me, aren't you? That's no dream. How many fingers do you see?

LUPE: Five.

LETICIA: Right! (*Grabs her face.*) Five fingers around your fat little face. You feel this?

LUPE: Yeah. Yeah.

LETICIA: That's what's real, 'manita. What you can see, taste, and touch . . . that's real.

LUPE: I still say, you can't know for sure.

LETICIA: Say something else. You're boring me. (*Lupe sits. Puts her shoes on.*)

LUPE: I went over to Cholo Park yesterday.

LETICIA: You better not tell Mom. Some chick jus' got her lonche down there the other day. They found her naked, man, all chopped up.

LUPE: Ooooh. Shaddup.

LETICIA: Well, it's true. What were you doing down there?

LUPE: Nut'ing. Jus' hanging out with Frances and her brother, Nacho.

LETICIA: God, I hate that huevón. Stupid cholo . . . he jus' hangs out with you guys cuz nobody his own age will have anything to do with him. (*Beat.*) So what were you guys up to?

LUPE: (*Humming.*) Nut'ing.

LETICIA: C'mon. Fess up! Out with it!

LUPE: Nut'ing. The boys were jus' throwing cats.

LETICIA: What?

LUPE: They was throwing cats off the hill.

LETICIA: What d'yuh mean?

LUPE: Well, they stand up there, grab the gatos by the colas and swing 'em above their heads and let 'em go. Ay, they let out such a grito! It's horrible! It sounds like a baby being killed!

LETICIA: And you watch that shit?

LUPE: They was the ones doing it . . . Most of the time the gatos land on their feet. But this one time this one got caught on these telephone wires. It jus' hung there in shock with its lengua así. (*She sticks out her tongue dramatically.*)

LETICIA: Ay, stop it! I swear you're really sick. How can you stand to see 'em do that?

LUPE: It's hard to take your eyes off it.

LETICIA: Si-ick. (*Holding her hair in place.*) Here, Lupe. Stick the bobby pin in for me.

LUPE: (*Taking the pin from Leticia.*) Where?

LETICIA: Back here. C'mon, my arm's getting tired. (*She does.*) Ouch! ¡Bruta! You want to draw blood or what?

Takunda
By Charles Smith

Takunda, 16; Chipo, 16

Charles Smith's *Takunda* weaves music and folk tales through the story of a young dark-skinned Shona girl's coming of age during a crucial year of civil unrest. Set in 1973 in a region of southern Africa, then known as Rhodesia, now Zimbabwe, the play concerns Takunda and her family, caught in the turmoil of political upheaval, informants, betrayal and social rejection. When the police arrest Takunda's father for conducting secret meetings of protest, the villagers turn against the family fearing implication and being identified as a rebel. Through it all, Takunda attempts to understand the complexities of sticking to one's beliefs and to maintain her girlhood friendship with Chipo. When it is made known that Takunda's father has been arrested, the affections of a young man, Fungi, toward Takunda change causing confusion and hurt. Finally, Takunda tests her own convictions by weighing her feelings regarding the current situation against the lessons learned from the Shona folk tales.

In the first scene, Chipo shows Takunda a secret meeting place. The "chuma" is a string of beads given in affection. Because the play is acted by an ensemble of players who take many roles, Chipo is here listed as "Woman/Chipo."

WOMAN/CHIPO: Damn it!

TAKUNDA: Chipo?

WOMAN/CHIPO: Come on.

TAKUNDA: What happened?

WOMAN/CHIPO: Just come with me, will you?

TAKUNDA: Where? Chipo? Where are we going? Chipo? (*They walk to another part of the stage.*) What place is this?

WOMAN/CHIPO: It's my secret place. My bako. I come here sometimes to be alone.

TAKUNDA: So why are we here?

WOMAN/CHIPO: I thought maybe you needed a place to be alone.

TAKUNDA: What happened with Fungi?

WOMAN/CHIPO: Takunda, they say your father was arrested.

TAKUNDA: So?

WOMAN/CHIPO: So was he?

TAKUNDA: They took him for questioning.

WOMAN/CHIPO: When?

TAKUNDA: Yesterday.

WOMAN/CHIPO: Takunda . . . why didn't you tell me?

TAKUNDA: I haven't had the chance.

WOMAN/CHIPO: Everybody in school has been talking about it.

TAKUNDA: I don't know why. They're going to release him.

WOMAN/CHIPO: Takunda, you should have told me!

TAKUNDA: When? I haven't seen you. When was I supposed to tell you?

WOMAN/CHIPO: I don't know.

TAKUNDA: Anyway, what's the big deal? I told you, they're going to release him.

WOMAN/CHIPO: When?

TAKUNDA: Soon.

WOMAN/CHIPO: Did they say that, Takunda?

TAKUNDA: Not in those words. But they're going to release him.

WOMAN/CHIPO: I hope so.

TAKUNDA: What's this with Fungi? You think that's the reason he took his chuma back?

WOMAN/CHIPO: I don't know.

TAKUNDA: Because of my father?

WOMAN/CHIPO: You can't try to figure boys out. You'll go mad like SaMuchena the Vendor.

TAKUNDA: He's afraid. Afraid because my father was arrested.

WOMAN/CHIPO: Will you forget about Fungi! He's kabenzi. A baboon. If he cared about you, he wouldn't let something like this deter him. He's a jellyfish, Takunda. A weak, spineless jellyfish.

TAKUNDA: He said he wanted to give me another chuma. One much larger, and prettier.

WOMAN/CHIPO: Well, if I were you, I wouldn't hold my breath.

TAKUNDA: God. He's a jellyfish.

WOMAN/CHIPO: I could have told you that a long time ago. (*Pause.*)

TAKUNDA: This is a good secret place you have here.

WOMAN/CHIPO: Thank you.

TAKUNDA: You can see out, but no one can see in.

WOMAN/CHIPO: You can come back if you like. Whenever you want. We both can come. We can meet here and talk . . .

TAKUNDA: You and I?

WOMAN/CHIPO: If you want.

TAKUNDA: I wouldn't want anyone else here.

WOMAN/CHIPO: Whatever you want.

TAKUNDA: Can we have a signal?

WOMAN/CHIPO: A what?

TAKUNDA: A signal, so we'll know when to meet.

WOMAN/CHIPO: We don't need a signal.

TAKUNDA: This is so close, you'll probably hear it over the entire area. How about this? Coooo! Coooo!

WOMAN/CHIPO: You sound like a frightened gazelle.

TAKUNDA: That's the idea. If you hear it, that means I'm here and you're to come immediately. And if I hear it, I'll come. Try it. Coooo!

WOMAN/CHIPO: I'm not doing that. It's stupid.

TAKUNDA: Come on, Chipo. Coooo!

WOMAN/CHIPO: Co.

TAKUNDA: You can do better than that! Coooo!

WOMAN/CHIPO: Coo.

TAKUNDA: Coooo!

WOMAN/CHIPO: Coooo!

TAKUNDA: That's it. Coooo!

WOMAN/CHIPO: Coooo!

TAKUNDA: Good. Whenever we want to meet, we'll give the signal.

WOMAN/CHIPO: No matter what time?

TAKUNDA: No matter what time. Day or night. Deal?

WOMAN/CHIPO: Deal.

TAKUNDA: Jellyfish.

WOMAN/CHIPO: Damn jellyfish.

TAKUNDA: Chipo?

WOMAN/CHIPO: Yeah?

TAKUNDA: Are you afraid?

WOMAN/CHIPO: Afraid of what?

TAKUNDA: The police.

WOMAN/CHIPO: Don't make me laugh.

TAKUNDA: You're not afraid of the police?

WOMAN/CHIPO: I wish Mapurisa would try to bother me. I'd give them what for and why.

TAKUNDA: No!

WOMAN/CHIPO: Yes! I'd fight them, with my fists and with my feet.

TAKUNDA: Chipo?

WOMAN/CHIPO: I'd kick them in their machende.

TAKUNDA: (*Grabbing her crotch.*) Ooooooooh!

WOMAN/CHIPO: And then pluck out their eyes!

TAKUNDA: (*Grabbing her eyes.*) Ooooooooh!

WOMAN/CHIPO: One thing you have to learn about me, Takunda. I am afraid of no one.

[MAN 2/FATHER'S VOICE: Chipo! Uri kupi!]

WOMAN/CHIPO: Oh God, except my father!

[MAN 2/FATHER'S VOICE: Chipo!]

WOMAN/CHIPO: I've got to go or he's going to kill me.

TAKUNDA: I'll see you tomorrow, Chipo.

[MAN 2/FATHER'S VOICE: Chipo!

WOMAN/CHIPO: Okay. Tomorrow!

(*Chipo runs off.*)

♦ ♦ ♦ ♦

Takunda, 16; Chipo, 16

In the second scene, Chipo shares her fears with Takunda.

TAKUNDA: (*Moving off.*) Cooo! Cooo! (*She pauses, waits for a response.*) Coooo! Coooo!

WOMAN/CHIPO: Taku?

TAKUNDA: Over here. What happened to you in school today?

WOMAN/CHIPO: My parents wouldn't let me go.

TAKUNDA: Why not?

WOMAN/CHIPO: They said it was too dangerous.

TAKUNDA: Dangerous?

WOMAN/CHIPO: They're afraid of a police raid. They say that some students are running off and joining the boys in the bush.

TAKUNDA: That's silly.

WOMAN/CHIPO: Hey, if it gets me out of English lessons, it's okay with me.

TAKUNDA: I saw Fungi today.

WOMAN/CHIPO: And what did Mr. Jellyfish have to say for himself?

TAKUNDA: Nothing. He was with his friend. He pretended as if he didn't see me.

WOMAN/CHIPO: Jellyfish.

TAKUNDA: You know what I think? I think Fungi gave his chuma to his friend. (*Chipo laughs, covers her mouth.*) It wouldn't surprise me. They're together all the time.

WOMAN/CHIPO: And that would explain everything.

TAKUNDA: Wouldn't surprise me one bit.

WOMAN/CHIPO: Has your father been released?

TAKUNDA: No.

WOMAN/CHIPO: It's been three days now.

TAKUNDA: I know how long it's been.

WOMAN/CHIPO: Aren't you worried?

TAKUNDA: No. My mother says they have no basis for his retention. She says they now have to wait for the most opportune time to minimize political embarrassment.

WOMAN/CHIPO: My father says the shit's going to hit the fan soon.

TAKUNDA: What does he mean, the shit's going to hit the fan?

WOMAN/CHIPO: Once the police get the names of the others who attended the meetings.

TAKUNDA: But my father is the only one with those names.

WOMAN/CHIPO: Ah, Takunda. Surely he'll give them to them.

TAKUNDA: But he won't.

WOMAN/CHIPO: Takunda . . . you don't know what they do to people.

TAKUNDA: I don't care what they do to people. My father is strong.

WOMAN/CHIPO: And my father says they'll get it out of him, one way or the other. And when they do, look out buddy boy.

TAKUNDA: What's this you're talking? You're just like all the rest of them. Like Fungi and Uncle Gibson. You're afraid.

WOMAN/CHIPO: I'm not afraid, Takunda.

TAKUNDA: You don't come to school anymore, I don't see you or talk to you, you're afraid.

WOMAN/CHIPO: I'm not afraid. I'm here now, aren't I?

TAKUNDA: Now. Here in your secret place. Your big-time secret place where no one can see us. That's why you brought me here, isn't it? You want to be my friend but you don't want anyone to know. So you bring me here to your secret place. Your big-time, nowhere, secret place.

WOMAN/CHIPO: I brought you here because I wanted to share it with you. I never brought anyone here before. Not David when he gave me his chuma, not my brothers or sister, no one. I feel good when I'm here. I wanted you to feel the same way. I'm sorry. (*She leaves.*)

SCENES
FOR
TWO MEN

The Dance And The Railroad
By David Henry Hwang

Lone, 20; Ma, 18

This two-character play by American playwright David Henry Hwang returns the writer to his heritage (he was born the son of Chinese immigrants). Lone and Ma are young "ChinaMan railroad workers" on the transcontinental railroad in the hot summer of 1867. Lone, visionary and artistic, knows the inhumanity and manipulation these workers face daily, while Ma can at first only see the potential for great wealth and a new start in this magical land of opportunity. Together, the unlikely two find ways of learning from each other.

In this scene, Ma discovers Lone on a mountaintop practicing movements for a Chinese opera.

MA: Hey.
LONE: You? Again?
MA: I forgive you.
LONE: You . . . what?
MA: For making fun of me yesterday. I forgive you.
LONE: You can't –
MA: No. Don't thank me.
LONE: You can't forgive me.
MA: No. Don't mention it.
LONE: You – ! I never asked for your forgiveness.
MA: I know. That's just the kind guy I am.
LONE: This is ridiculous. Why don't you leave? Go down to your
    friends and play soldiers, sing songs, tell stories.
MA: Ah! See? That's just it. I got other ways I wanna spend my
    time. Will you teach me the opera?
LONE: What?
MA: I wanna learn it. I dreamt about it all last night.
LONE: No.
MA: The dance, the opera – I can do it.
LONE: You think so?

MA: Yeah. When I get outa here, I wanna go back to China and perform.

LONE: You want to become an actor?

MA: Well, I wanna perform.

LONE: Don't you remember the story about the three sons whose parents send them away to learn a trade? After three years, they return. The first one says, "I have become a coppersmith." The parents say, "Good. Second son, what have you become?" "I've become a silversmith." "Good – and youngest son, what about you?" "I have become an actor." When the parents hear that their son has become only an actor, they are very sad. The mother beats her head against the ground until the ground, out of pity, opens up and swallows her. The father is so angry he can't even speak, and the anger builds up inside him until it blows his body to pieces—little bits of his skin are found hanging from trees days later. You don't know how you endanger your relatives by becoming an actor.

MA: Well, I don't wanna become an "actor." That sounds terrible. I just wanna perform. Look, I'll be rich by the time I get out of here, right?

LONE: Oh?

MA: Sure. By the time I go back to China, I'll ride in gold sedan chairs, with twenty wives fanning me all around.

LONE: Twenty wives? This boy is ambitious.

MA: I'll give out pigs on New Year's and keep a stable of small birds to give to any woman who pleases me. And in my spare time, I'll perform.

LONE: Between your twenty wives and your birds, where will you find a free moment?

MA: I'll play Gwan Gung and tell stories of what life was like on the Gold Mountain.

LONE: Ma, just how long have you been in "America"?

MA: Huh? About four weeks.

LONE: You are a big dreamer.

MA: Well, all us ChinaMen here are – right? Men with little

dreams—have little brains to match. They walk with their eyes down, trying to find extra grains of rice on the ground.

LONE: So, you know all about "America"? Tell me, what kind of stories will you tell?

MA: I'll say, "We laid tracks like soldiers. Mountains? We hung from cliffs in baskets and winds blew us like birds. Snow? We lived underground like moles for days at a time. Deserts? We – "

LONE: Wait. Wait. How do you know these things after only four weeks?

MA: They told me – the other ChinaMen on the gang. We've been telling stories ever since the strike began.

LONE: They make it sound like it's very enjoyable.

MA: They said it is.

LONE: Oh? And you believe them?

MA: They're my friends. Living underground in winter – sounds exciting, huh?

LONE: Did they say anything about the cold?

MA: Oh, I already know about that. They told me about the mild winters and the warm snow.

LONE: Warm snow?

MA: When I go home, I'll bring some back to show my brothers.

LONE: Bring some – ? On the boat?

MA: They'll be shocked – they never seen American snow before.

LONE: You can't. By the time you get snow to the boat, it'll have melted, evaporated, and returned as rain already.

MA: No.

LONE: No?

MA: Stupid.

LONE: Me?

MA: You been here awhile, haven't you?

LONE: Yes. Two years.

MA: Then how come you're so stupid? This is the Gold Mountain. The snow here doesn't melt. It's not wet.

LONE: That's what they told you?

MA: Yeah. It's true.

LONE: Did anyone show you any of this snow?

MA: No. It's not winter.

LONE: So where does it go?

MA: Huh?

LONE: Where does it go, if it doesn't melt? What happens to it?

MA: The snow? I dunno. I guess it just stays around.

LONE: So where is it? Do you see any?

MA: Here? Well, no, but . . . (*Pause.*) This is probably one of those places where it doesn't snow – even in winter.

LONE: Oh.

MA: Anyway, what's the use of me telling you what you already know? Hey, c'mon – teach me some of that stuff. Look – I've been practicing the walk – how's this? (*Demonstrates.*)

LONE: You look like a duck in heat.

MA: Hey – it's a start, isn't it?

LONE: Tell you what – you want to play some *die siu?*

MA: *Die siu?* Sure.

LONE: You know, I'm pretty good.

MA: Hey, I play with the guys at camp. You can't be any better than Lee – he's really got it down.
    (*Lone pulls out a case with two dice.*)

LONE: I used to play till morning.

MA: Hey, us too. We see the sun start to rise, and say, "Hey, if we got to sleep now, we'll never get up for work." So we just keep playing.

LONE: (*Holding out dice.*) *Die* or *siu?*

MA: *Siu.*

LONE: You sure?

MA: Yeah!

LONE: All right. (*He rolls.*) *Die*!

MA: *Siu!*
    (*They see the result.*)
    Not bad.
    (*They continue taking turns rolling through the following section; Ma always loses.*)

LONE: I haven't touched these in two years.

MA: I gotta practice more.

LONE: Have you lost much money?

MA: Huh? So what?

LONE: Oh, you have gold hidden in all your shirt linings, huh?

MA: Here in "America" – losing is no problem. You know – End of the Year Bonus?

LONE: Oh, right.

MA: After I get that, I'll laugh at what I lost.

LONE: Lee told you there was a bonus, right?

MA: How'd you know?

LONE: When I arrived here, Lee told me there was a bonus, too.

MA: Lee teach you how to play?

LONE: Him? He talked to me a lot.

MA: Look, why don't you come down and start playing with the guys again?

LONE: "The guys."

MA: Before we start playing, Lee uses a stick to write "Kill!" in the dirt.

LONE: You seem to live for your nights with "the guys."

MA: What's life without friends, huh?

LONE: Well, why do *you* think I stopped playing?

MA: Hey, maybe you were the one getting killed, huh?

LONE: What?

MA: Hey, just kidding.

LONE: Who's getting killed here?

MA: Just a joke.

LONE: That's not a joke, it's blasphemy.

MA: Look, obviously you stopped playing 'cause you wanted to practice the opera.

LONE: Do you understand that discipline?

MA: But, I mean, you don't have to overdo it either. You don't have to treat 'em like dirt. I mean, who are you trying to impress?

(*Pause. Lone throws dice into the bushes.*)

LONE: Ooooops. Better go see who won.

MA: Hey! C'mon! Help me look!

LONE: If you find them, they are yours.

MA: You serious?

LONE: Yes?

MA: Here. (*Finds the dice.*)

LONE: Who won?

MA: I didn't check.

LONE: Well, no matter. Keep the dice. Take them and go play with your friends.

MA: Here. (*He offers them to Lone.*) A present.

LONE: A present? This isn't a present!

MA: They're mine, aren't they? You gave them to me, right?

LONE: Well, yes, but –

MA: So now I'm giving them to you.

LONE: You can't give me a present. I don't want them.

MA: You wanted them enough to keep them two years.

LONE: I'd forgotten I had them.

MA: See, I know, Lone. You wanna get rid of me. But you can't. I'm paying for lessons.

LONE: With my dice.

MA: Mine now. (*He offers them again.*) Here.

(*Pause. Lone runs Ma's hand across his forehead.*)

LONE: Feel this.

MA: Hey!

LONE: Pretty wet, huh?

MA: Big deal.

LONE: Well, it's not from playing *die siu.*

MA: I know how to sweat. I wouldn't be here if I didn't.

LONE: Yes, but are you willing to sweat after you've finished sweating? Are you willing to come up after you've spent the whole day chipping half an inch off a rock, and punish your body some more?

MA: Yeah. Even after work, I still –

LONE: No, you don't. You want to gamble, and tell dirty stories, and dress up like women to do shows.

MA: Hey, I never did that.

LONE: You've only been here a month. (*Pause.*) And what about "the guys"? They're not going to treat you so well once you stop playing with them. Are you willing to work all day listening to them whisper, "That one – let's put spiders in his soup"?

MA: They won't do that to me. With you, it's different.

LONE: Is it?

MA: You don't have to act that way.

LONE: What way?

MA: Like you're so much better than them.

LONE: No. You haven't even begun to understand. To practice every day, you must have a fear to force you up here.

MA: A fear? No – it's 'cause what you're doing is beautiful.

LONE: No.

MA: I've seen it.

LONE: It's ugly to practice when the mountain has turned your muscles to ice. When my body hurts too much to come here, I look at the other ChinaMen and think, "They are dead. Their muscles work only because the white man forces them. I live because I can still force my muscles to work for me." Say it, "They are dead."

MA: No. They're my friends.

LONE: Well, then, take your dice down to your friends.

MA: But I want to learn –

LONE: This is your first lesson.

MA: Look, it shouldn't matter –

LONE: It does.

MA: It shouldn't matter what I think.

LONE: Attitude is everything.

MA: But as long as I come up, do the exercises –

LONE: I'm not going to waste time on a quitter.

MA: I'm not!

LONE: Then say it. – "They are dead men."

MA: I can't.

LONE: Then you will never have the dedication.

MA: That doesn't prove anything.

LONE: I will not teach a dead man.

MA: What?

LONE: If you can't see it, then you're dead too.

MA: Don't start pinning –

LONE: Say it!

MA: All right.

LONE: What?

MA: All right. I'm one of them. I'm a dead man too.
    (*Pause.*)

LONE: I thought as much. So, go. You have your friends.

MA: But I don't have a teacher.

LONE: I don't think you need both.

MA: Are you sure?

LONE: I'm being questioned by a child.
    (*Lone returns to practicing. Silence.*)

MA: Look, Lone, I'll come up here every night – after work – I'll
    spend my time practicing, okay? (*Pause.*) But I'm not gonna
    say that they're dead. Look at them. They're on strike; dead
    men don't go on strike, Lone. The white devils – they try and
    stick us with a ten-hour day. We want a return to eight hours
    and also a fourteen-dollar-a-month raise. I learned the demon
    English – listen: "Eight hour a day good for white man, all
    same good for ChinaMan." These are the demands of Live
    ChinaMen, Lone. Dead men don't complain.

LONE: All right, this is something new. No one can judge the
    ChinaMen till after the strike.

MA: They say we'll hold out for months if we have to. The smart
    men will live on what we've hoarded.

LONE: A ChinaMan's mouth can swallow the earth. (*He takes the
    dice.*) While the strike is on, I'll teach you.

MA: And afterwards?

LONE: Afterwards – we'll decide then whether these are dead or
    live men.

MA: When can we start?

LONE: We've already begun. Give me your hand.

The Dybbuk
By S. Ansky; Translated by Henry G. Alsberg and Winifred Katzin

Chennoch, 18-20; Channon, 18-20

The Dybbuk recounts the tragic love of Channon and Leah. Having been denied Leah's hand in marriage by her father in favor of a wealthier suitor, Channon turns to the magic of Kabala in hopes of winning her love but dies in the mystical attempt. In death, Channon returns as a Dybbuk – or evil spirit, and possesses Leah's body on her wedding day.

In the scene below, Channon shares with his friend Chennoch his views about sin and the afterlife.

CHENNOCH: (*Looks up from his book, attentively at Channon.*) Channon! You go about dreaming all the time.

CHANNON: (*Moves away from the Ark, and slowly approaches Chennoch, standing before him, lost in thought.*) Nothing – nothing but secrets and symbols – and the right path is not to be found. (*Short pause.*) Krasny is the name of the village . . . and the miracle-man's name is Rabbi Elchannon . . .

CHENNOCH: What's that you're saying?

CHANNON: (*As if waking out of a trance.*) I? Nothing. I was only thinking.

CHENNOCH: (*Shaking his head.*) You've been meddling with the Kabala, Channon. Ever since you came back, you haven't had a book in your hand.

CHANNON: (*Not understanding.*) Not had a book in my hand? What book do you mean?

CHENNOCH: The Talmud of course – the Laws. You know very well . . .

CHANNON: (*Still in his dreams.*) Talmud? The Laws? Never had them in my hand? The Talmud is cold and dry . . . so are the Laws. (*Comes to himself suddenly. He speaks with animation.*) Under the earth's surface, Chennoch, there is a world exactly the same as ours upon it, with fields and forests, seas and deserts, cities and villages. Storms rage over the deserts and over the seas upon which sail great ships. And over the dense forests, reverberating with the roll of thunder, eternal fear holds sway. Only in the absence of one thing does that world differ from ours. There is no sky, from which the sun pours down its burning heat and bolts of fire fall . . . So it is with the Talmud. It is deep and glorious and vast. But it chains you to the earth – it forbids you to attempt the heights. (*With enthusiasm.*) But the Kabala, the Kabala tears your soul away from earth and lifts you to the realms of the highest heights. Spreads all the heavens out before your eyes, and leads direct to Pardes,* reaches out in the infinite, and raises a corner of the great curtain itself. (*Collapses.*) My heart turns faint – I have no strength . . .

CHENNOCH: (*Solemnly.*) That is all true. But you forget that those ecstatic flights into the upper regions are fraught with the utmost peril, for it is there that you are likely to come to grief and hurl yourself into the deepest pit below. The Talmud raises the soul toward the heights by slow degrees, but keeps guard over it like a faithful sentinel, who neither sleeps nor dreams. The Talmud clothes the soul with an armor of steel and keeps it ever on the straight path, so that it stray neither to the right nor to the left. But the Kabala . . . Remember what the Talmud says: (*He chants the following in the manner of Talmudic recitation.*) Four reached Pardes. Ben Azzai, Ben Zoma, Acher and Rabbi Akiva. Ben Azzai looked within and died. Ben Zoma looked within and lost his reason. Acher renounced the fundamentals of all belief. Rabbi Akiva alone went in and came out again unscathed.

CHANNON: Don't try to frighten me with them. We don't know how they went, nor with what. They may have failed because they went to look and not to offer themselves as a sacrifice. But others went after them – that we know. Holy Ari and the Holy Balshem.** They did not fail.

* *Paradise,* **The founder of the Chassidic sect, known as the Basht.*

CHENNOCH: Are you comparing yourself to them?

CHANNON: To nobody. I go my own way.

CHENNOCH: What sort of way is that?

CHANNON: You wouldn't understand.

CHENNOCH: I wish to and I will. My soul, too, is drawn toward the high planes.

CHANNON: (*After a moment's reflection.*) The service of our holy men consists in cleansing human souls, tearing away the sin that clings to them and raising them to the shining source whence they come. Their work is very difficult because sin is ever lurking at the door. No sooner is one soul cleansed than another comes in its place, more sin-corroded still. No sooner is one generation brought to repentance than the next one appears, more stiff-necked than the last. And as each generation grows weaker, its sins become stronger, and the holy men fewer and fewer.

CHENNOCH: Then, according to your philosophy, what ought to be done?

CHANNON: (*Quietly, but with absolute conviction.*) There is no need to wage war on sin. All that is necessary is to burn it away, as the goldsmith refines gold in his powerful flame; as the farmer winnows the grain from the chaff. So must sin be refined of its uncleanness, until only its holiness remains.

CHENNOCH: (*Astonished.*) Holiness in sin? How do you make that out?

CHANNON: Everything created by God contains a spark of holiness.

CHENNOCH: Sin was not created by God but by Satan.

CHANNON: And who created Satan? God. Since he is the antithesis of God, he is an aspect of God, and therefore must contain also a germ of holiness.

CHENNOCH: (*Crushed.*) Holiness in Satan? I can't . . . I don't understand . . . Let me think . . . (*His head sinks into his hands, propped up by both elbows on the desk. There is a pause.*)

CHANNON: (*Stands beside him and in a trembling voice, bending down to reach his ear.*) Which sin is the strongest of all?

Which one is the hardest to conquer? The sin of lust for a woman, isn't it?

CHENNOCH: (*Without raising his head.*) Yes.

CHANNON: And when you have cleansed this sin in a powerful flame, then this greatest uncleanness becomes the greatest holiness. It becomes "The Song of Songs." (*He holds his breath.*) The Song of Songs. (*Drawing himself up, he begins to chant in a voice which, though subdued, is charged with rapture.*) "Behold thou art fair, my love. Thou hast dove's eyes within they locks; thy hair is as a flock of goats that appear from Mount Gilead. Thy teeth are like a flock of sheep that are even shorn, which came up from the washing; whereof every one bear twins and none barren among them."

The House of Ramon Iglesia
By José Rivera

Charlie, 16; Javier, 22

The New York Ensemble Studio Theatre first produced *The House of Ramon Iglesia,* which was a winner of the Foundation of the Dramatists Guild/CBS Play Contest. Set in Holbrook, Long Island, New York, this contemporary play depicts the daily life of the Iglesias, a Puerto Rican family struggling to make ends meet. The play's power derives from the tension between the father and the eldest son, Javier, who is attempting to break away from his immigrant heritage. In the end, Javier comes to realize that as an Hispanic-American, he must first learn to appreciate his ethnic heritage before he can find his true identity.

In Scene 3 of Act One, Javier discovers his younger brother, Charlie, packing up the family's belongings; Ramon plans on taking the family home to Puerto Rico.

There are half-filled boxes all over the living room, piles of clothes, and garbage. The walls are nearly bare and some of the clutter of the room has been relieved. Charlie is playing a radio and packing things into boxes. Javier enters, putting a shirt on.

JAVIER: *Charlie . . .*

CHARLIE: Carlos to you, bro.

JAVIER: *Charlie . . .*

CHARLIE: It's Carlos now.

JAVIER: (*Noticing the boxes.*) When are you going to learn to *spell?*

CHARLIE: What? I can spell.

JAVIER: Did you mark up all the boxes like this? (*Inspects the other boxes.*)

CHARLIE: That's the spelling I got from Mom.

JAVIER: "That's the spelling I got from Mom."

CHARLIE: Hey, you better watch your step, when Julio leaves, *I'm* the beast of the house!

JAVIER: How the hell do you figure that . . . *Charlie?*

CHARLIE: 'Cause I got these. (*Grabs crotch.*) I don't know what you got!

JAVIER: None of you guys have a method for anything. Look at this mess. I wish you guys would check with me before doing stuff like this.

CHARLIE: What stuff?

JAVIER: Sending half your clothes to Doña Perez. Getting rid of half the furniture.

CHARLIE: If we listened to you, we'd never leave.

JAVIER: You guys just go ahead and do these mindless things.

CHARLIE: "You guys."

JAVIER: (*Sitting down to write letters.*) I mean, I didn't know Dad quit his job last week. No one told me.

CHARLIE: He was afraid you'd have a hemorrhage.

JAVIER: Wouldn't you? Charlie, Dad's spent Calla's downpayment already. What's he going to do for cash after it's gone?

CHARLIE: After today, Calla can pay Dad the balance on the house.

JAVIER: That's not the point. It's just that you guys never plan properly.

CHARLIE: (*Crossing to Javier.*) Why do you call everybody "you guys"? It really sucks, Javier. You're part of this family too, you know.

JAVIER: Don't remind me.

CHARLIE: You try to make everybody in the family feel stupid.

JAVIER: I don't try – it just happens. (*Charlie gives him a dirty look.*) I'm sorry Charlie – Carlos – whoever you are this week. I just wish you guys would consult with me sometimes.

CHARLIE: Consult with you! We have trouble eating meals with you.

JAVIER: Where did I go wrong? Where did I fail?

CHARLIE: You went wrong by calling everybody in the family "you guys." (*They continue packing boxes.*) Man, I don't know where you get all your hemorrhoids from. This is the best thing that could happen to Mom and Dad.

JAVIER: To Mom, maybe.

CHARLIE: You don't go shopping with Mom – me and Dad got to talk to everybody in the store for her. She don't read English. Dad drives her everywhere. This place is worse than San Quentin to her.

JAVIER: It's her own fault. She could have learned English: she still can.

CHARLIE: I think it's neat she don't know English.

JAVIER: Doesn't know English.

CHARLIE: It's pure of her. And I think it would be great if you got happy for them, encourage them – .

JAVIER: I don't like encouraging people to quit – .

CHARLIE: I mean, Dad wanted to go back five years ago, but he said, "No, Javier's got to go to college first."

JAVIER: Am I going to be tormented because of my education?

CHARLIE: Because you forgot where it came from!

JAVIER: It came from *me* buddyboy – *me*, busting my ass, seeking out financial aid. If I hadn't taken the time to ask the right – .

CHARLIE: And where'd you get the time? From Dad!

JAVIER: Oh Christ . . .

CHARLIE: *Dad*, who went around ripped-up and filthy-dirty because he worked two jobs so you wouldn't have to work *any*. Dad bent down to clean floors so you'd be able to . . . to . . . walk all over his back, wipe your feet, and go . . . (*They work for a few moments longer.*) Anyway, I think Puerto Rico will be fun. Jungles and farms – you can't get that in Holbrook. And Mom says we can buy a horse down there – something else you can't get in Holbrook.

JAVIER: You can't get malaria in Holbrook either . . .

CHARLIE: . . . and hang out at the beach all day long . . .

JAVIER: . . . or tarantulas and hurricanes . . .

CHARLIE: . . . and all those pretty girls to fall in love with.

JAVIER: Early marriage, lots of brats, and a fat middle age!

CHARLIE: Racist!

JAVIER: (*Laughing.*) Mom hates it when she asks, "Why don't you marry a nice Latin girl?" and I always say back, "Nice Latin girls are fat and mean by the time they're twenty-nine."

CHARLIE: Mom thinks that . . . you really dislike our people.

JAVIER: Is that how it looks?

CHARLIE: Well. Yeah. I mean, you hardly speak Spanish anymore, you don't kiss Dad . . .

JAVIER: Charlie, I love you guys, you know I do. It's just "our people" I don't know about. I don't even know what "our people" even *means*. Is it some mass of Latin Americans on Eighth Avenue? Is it all the Puerto Ricans hanging out on Avenue D? Christ, it's so weird! Whenever I see some poor old Puerto Rican stumbling around drunk, acting like a fool, I think of Dad. If I see a bunch of guys with their numb-chucks and radios, I think of our cousins, I mean, I know exactly how these people think, what they like and dislike, what they need . . . and something in me feels like its got to help them . . . and I will someday . . . but for now, I just want to be as far away as possible.

Once Upon A Dream
By Miguel González-Pando

Machito, 20; Tony, 20

Set in New York City, *Once Upon A Dream* explores the world of Hispanic exiles and refugees struggling to build a life in the urban world far removed from their Caribbean origins. We encounter the widowed mother, Dolores Jiménez, and her family, each of whom is tossed and torn between his or her native culture and the obstacles they confront in the city. Throughout the play fantasy and nostalgia confront the cold realities of the present and force the characters to rediscover who they are.

In thefollowing scene, Machito and his friend Tony celebrate their luck at the horse races.

◆ ◆ ◆ ◆

It is about 3:00 a.m. Tony is sitting on the fire escape window sill; at his side, almost with his back to Tony, is Machito, balancing precariously on a chair leaning against the wall. The apartment is dark, except for the flashing blue light of a neon sign coming through the window and directly illuminating Machito's face. Both are drinking beer.

TONY: (*Laughing.*) . . . and just when I was beginning to think it was hopeless and we'd laid down our last buck on a lame horse – I swear, Machito, I'd just about given up – then, wow! from way back, number one, our Pretty Baby, suddenly seems to wake up as he comes out of the last turn . . . (*Sips his beer.*) Hell, then he really took off like the wind!

MACHITO: (*Imitating the race announcer and pretending to ride a horse.*) " . . . and on the final stretch, number one, Pretty Baby, catches up with Bet on Me and begins to gain on the two leaders, Blue Grass and Canonero . . . and with a quarter-mile to go, it's Canonero first, Blue Grass second, followed by Pretty Baby in third place . . . " But our Pretty Baby advances and fights for second place with Blue Grass . . . "and now, it's Canonero first, followed closely by Blue Grass and Pretty Baby . . . " (*Tony, "riding" on the window sill, cheers Pretty Baby on.*) "And Pretty Baby finally catches Blue Grass, and with just a few yards to go, it's Canonero and Pretty Baby running neck-to-neck . . . " (*Increasingly excited, Tony keeps cheering Pretty Baby on.*) "Canonero and Pretty Baby . . . Canonero and Pretty Baby . . . and at the post it's . . . "

TONY: (*Raising his arms in the air like a victorious jockey at the finish line.*) . . . The winner by a nose, number one, Pretty Baby . . . making us fucking rich! (*Drinks from his beer can.*)

MACHITO: Did I tell you or what?

TONY: Man, you practically never miss . . .

MACHITO: (*Proudly.*) The magic formula can't fail: dreaming at noon . . . shit . . . horses . . . the itch in the palms of my hands when I wake up . . . What else could that little horse of mine do but win?

TONY: Hey, Machito, about that dream . . . how did you figure it out?

MACHITO: The formula . . . the magic formula: one horse and three mountains – the number one horse in the third race . . .

TONY: Maybe it was the other way around: the number three horse in the first race?

MACHITO: (*Hiding his amusement at Tony's naïveté.*) Tony, how the hell could it be the first race, when we didn't get to the racetrack until the end of the second race . . . ? Don't you see?

TONY: Hell, you're right, what a dumb question . . . !

MACHITO: It's easier than it looks . . . when you have this magic power, of course . . . Want another beer?

TONY: I'll get it . . . I'll get it . . .

MACHITO: (*Going to the refrigerator.*) Better let me do it: you may stumble in the dark and wake up the old lady, then we'll end up having to listen to that stupid nagging of hers: "What are you doing still up in the middle of the night?" (*Opens the refrigerator and takes out two beers.*) Talk to me!

TONY: What . . . ?

MACHITO: Catch! (*Hurls a can of beer towards Tony.*)

TONY: Hell, you sure are something, bro'!

MACHITO: (*Faking a mysterious tone.*) That's another of my supernatural powers: finding beer cans in the dark – they don't call me the Wizard of Darkness for nothing. (*Laughs.*) Check this out! Check this out – with my eyes closed . . . (*Runs around the room confidently, then gets back to the chair; sits down and opens the can of beer.*) Am I the Wizard of Darkness or what . . . ? (*Takes a sip of beer, amused.*) And you ain't seen nothing yet: you gotta see me shave with the razor my father left me.

TONY: (*Raising his beer can.*) Let's drink to Pretty Baby, number one in the third race! (*Drinks.*)

MACHITO: Here's to Pretty Baby, number one in the third race!

TONY: . . . and how did you know it was the Belmont Racetrack and not the one at . . . ?

MACHITO: (*Pretending annoyance.*) Hey, enough of that! Whatcha trying to do – steal the secrets from the Wizard of Darkness? (*Holding back his laughter.*)

TONY: (*Naïvely.*) No, no, Machito, I swear I'm not, I swear I'm not!

MACHITO: Look, you better stick to counting the money: I'm the one with the magic powers around here, okay?

TONY: Five hundred dollars . . . five hundred fucking dollars . . . !

MACHITO: And if only the old lady had lent me a hundred instead of fifty fucking dollars, we'd still be counting, bro' . . .

TONY: A thousand, Machito! We could've won a thousand!

MACHITO: (*Breathing deep.*) A thousand dollars . . . (*Drinks.*) And what would you do with a thousand dollars, Tony?

TONY: I don't know, I don't know . . . I gotta think about it. (*Takes a sip of beer.*) Ah, now I know: I'd get drunk every day for a whole year. (*Laughs.*) No, no, no . . . better still . . . I think I better buy me . . . a Cadillac convertible. Second hand, but a real Cadillac! (*Takes a sip.*) What about you, Machito?

MACHITO: Me? Easy – I'd bet it all on my next dream.

TONY: You mean that, Machito . . . ? Wouldn't you like to get yourself a Cadillac . . . ?

MACHITO: What the hell would I do with a fucking Cadillac when I ain't got the money to pay for a driver?

TONY: I'll drive it for you . . . we'll buy it between the both of us, so I can keep on taking you around.

MACHITO: (*Pause.*) You really expect me to settle for just one thousand? Not for one thousand, not for ten thousand . . . not even for a hundred thousand . . . ! (*Pressing the cold beer can against his brow.*) I got ambitions, Tony . . . big ambitions, much bigger than you could guess – and my dreams are gonna take me all the way to the top. To the very top – no stopping, no looking back, like my old man did.

TONY: You bet, Machito!

MACHITO: (*Standing on the chair and raising the beer can high.*) And when fortune carries me to the highest peak, then I'll be ready to buy all the fucking Cadillacs I want, and hire me a bunch of dames with great big tits to drive me around.

TONY: No, Machito, no, I'm your driver. You gotta give me your word that I'll drive your Cadillac . . . I'll be the one to tell you what's going on around you . . .

MACHITO: (*Sits down again, thoughtfully, sipping his beer.*) Wanna know the truth? Things like that don't turn me on that much. But when I hit it big no one will ever feel sorry for me any more, no one will give a fuck about my being blind or a Spic with an accent! (*Takes a sip.*) Then I can buy the old lady a house to get her out of this fucking place and really show her who I am . . .

TONY: (*Fantasizing.*) Wow! – you and me driving all over the *barrio* in our Cadillac convertible. (*Proposing a toast.*) Here's to the Wizard of Darkness . . . !

MACHITO: (*Raises his beer can, but remains lost in his own thoughts for a moment.*) All I need is one good dream . . . (*Talking to himself.*) Just one good dream, and lots of money to bet on it . . . (*Takes a sip, thoughtfully.*) You believe in miracles, bro' . . . ?

TONY: Miracles? Like a dog learning to sing . . . ?

MACHITO: The real miracle is for the dog to bark, bro' . . . Check it out: we already got birds to do the fucking singing.

TONY: There ain't no fucking miracles, man . . .

MACHITO: Some lucky son-of-a-bitch hits the big jackpot every day.

Ain't that a miracle?

Tony: (*Unaware that he is reading Machito's mind.*) Machito, just think, all the dough we could've won if we'd bet your old lady's fifteen thousand . . .

Machito: (*Feeling found out, Machito loses his balance and topples over, chair and all, making a loud noise; both young men remain speechless.*)

Tony: You okay?

[Dolores: (*Turning on the light as she comes out of the bedroom, still half-asleep.*) Ay, you scared me to death! For God's sake, do you know what time it is? It's three o'clock in the morning! What are you doing still up? No, no, no . . . you don't have to tell me: you're getting drunk.]

Machito: We're celebrating!

Tony: Making a toast!

Machito: (*Loudly, raising his beer can.*) Here's to Pretty Baby, number one in the third race . . . !

Take A Giant Step
By Louis Peterson

Iggie, 17; Spence, 17

Take A Giant Step depicts the coming of age of Spence, a young African-American boy who experiences a sense of estrangement from his white friends as he emerges into adulthood. Confused by the prejudices of the adult world, his anger leads to his expulsion from school and a series of low life encounters that leave him even more bewildered. It is not until he has a confrontation with his parents, confides his fears in the family maid, and experiences the death of his grandmother that he is able to make sense of what he may become.

Here in Act One, Scene 1, Spence, who has just been kicked out of school, dreads the moment that his mother and father return home.

SPENCE: Dear, dear God – if that's my mother, just kill me as I open the door. (*Crosses to door. He hides a suitcase Left of piano. Opens door.*) Hi! Iggie – did you give me a scare!

IGGIE: Hiya, Spence.

SPENCE: I'm in a terrible hurry, Iggie. What do you want?

IGGIE: I just came over to see if you have any stamps to trade.

SPENCE: (*Crosses Left, gets shoes.*) I haven't got much time. Come on in – but you can't stay long. I've got to go somewhere.

IGGIE: (*Comes in.*) Where are you going?

SPENCE: No place. (*Pause.*) You sure you came over to trade stamps?

IGGIE: (*At sofa.*) Sure – that's what I came over for. I finished my home work early – so I thought I might –

SPENCE: (*Sits in chair Left of table.*) You know, Iggie – you're going to be out of school for a week. You didn't have to get your homework done so soon. That's the most disgusting thing I ever heard.

IGGIE: (*Crosses to table.*) Now look, if I want to get my homework done – that's my business. I don't tell you it's disgusting when you don't get yours done at all, do I?

SPENCE: (*Crosses back to sofa.*) O.K., O.K., Iggie. I only thought you came over because you heard I got kicked out of school.

IGGIE: No, Spence – I hadn't heard.

SPENCE: You're sure?

IGGIE: I told you I hadn't heard, didn't I? (*Sits right of table.*)

SPENCE: (*Crosses Right to close door.*) That kind of news has a way of getting around. (*Looking at him.*) Well, what are you thinking about? (*Crosses back to sofa.*)

IGGIE: Nothing. I was just thinking that if I got kicked out of school, I guess I'd just as soon I dropped dead right there on the floor in the principal's office.

SPENCE: O.K., Iggie. You don't need to rub it in. I get the picture. (*Looks upstairs.*)

IGGIE: I'm sorry, Spence. Is there anything I can do?

SPENCE: Now, Iggie – pardon me for being so damn polite – but what in the hell could you do about it?

IGGIE: I only want to help, Spence.

SPENCE: (*Crosses Left to below table.*) Well, you can't – so let's drop it, shall we?

IGGIE: I didn't mean that business about dropping dead. I probably wouldn't drop dead anyway. There's nothing wrong with my heart.

SPENCE: (*Sits sofa.*) Iggie – will you please cut it out.

IGGIE: Anything you say. I didn't mean to offend you.

SPENCE: You didn't offend me, Iggie. You just talk too much – that's all.

IGGIE: I'll try to do better in the future.

SPENCE: Look, Iggie – I've gone and hurt your feelings – haven't I? Hell – I'm sorry. I've always liked you, Iggie. You're a good kid. I'm apologizing, Iggie.

IGGIE: It's O.K., Spence. I know you're upset.

SPENCE: (*Crosses Down Left.*) I know how sensitive you are and all that and I just mow into you like crazy. I wish someone would tell me to shut my mouth. (*He walks to the stairs.*) Gram – hurry up with that dough, will you. Iggie – look – I'll tell you what I'm going to do for you. (*He goes over to the piano and comes back with his stamp album.*) Here – Iggie – it's yours. I want you to have it – because you're my friend.

IGGIE: Your album! But don't you want it, Spence?

SPENCE: No, Iggie. I don't want it.

IGGIE: But why? I think you must be crazy? (*Stands.*)

SPENCE: Hell, Iggie – because I'm growing up. I'm becoming a man, Iggie. And since I'm going out in just a few minutes with my girl friend – you know it's time for me to quit fooling around with stuff like that

IGGIE: Have you got a girl friend?

SPENCE: Yeh! Yes – I have – as a matter of fact I might get married soon. Forget all about school and all.

IGGIE: Really. Who is the girl, Spence?

SPENCE: Just a girl – that's all. And if everything works out O.K., I won't be coming back. You know, I'll have to get a job and stuff like that. Now you've got to go, Iggie, 'cause I've got to finish packing and get dressed. (*Leads Iggie Center.*)

IGGIE: Where are you going, Spence?

SPENCE: I can't tell you, Iggie.

IGGIE: Are you sure you're feeling all right?

SPENCE: Yes, Iggie, I'm feeling all right.

IGGIE: (*Crossing to door.*) Thank you for the gift. I appreciate it.

SPENCE: Forget it.

IGGIE: It's a beautiful album.

SPENCE: It certainly is.

IGGIE: (*Crosses to Center.*) Hey, I was just thinking – maybe I could go up and talk to old Hasbrook. It might do some good.

SPENCE: (*Crosses to door.*) I don't care about that any more, Iggie. I'm pretty sure I won't be coming back to school.

IGGIE: Are you sure you want me to have this, Spence?

SPENCE: Yes, Iggie, I want you to have it.

IGGIE: (*Crossing to door.*) Well – I hope I'll see you soon. (*He is opening the door.*)

SPENCE: (*At door.*) Hey, Iggie! You won't mind if just once in a while – I come over and see how you're doing with it?

IGGIE: I hope you will. Goodbye. (*Exits.*)

SPENCE: Geez – I don't know what's wrong with me. I think maybe my brains are molding or something. (*Gets suitcase, shoves clothes inside and runs upstairs.*) Hey, Gram – will you hurry up with that five bucks so I can get the hell out of here before I really do something desperate!

Welcome Home Jacko
By Mustapha Matura

Zippy, 17-21; Jacko, 20-25

Mustapha Matura, perhaps the leading dramatist of West Indian origin, wrote *Welcome Home Jacko* after visiting a community youth center in Sheffield, England. The center was a place for young people to socialize apart from the pangs of social oppression and racism. The play, set in just such a center, concerns a group of young people struggling for a Black identity. As the four young West Indians interact in the Club, exploring their place in the world, they assert their beliefs. Sandy, the white girl who manages the club, is preparing to welcome home Jacko, who has spent the last five years in prison for raping a girl.

In the scene below, Zippy, a West Indian, in a Rastafarian robe, is left alone to visit with Jacko.

ZIPPY: Cha, hey brother how yer like dem robes?

JACKO: Dey look nice.

ZIPPY: If yer ask Sandy she a make yer one too.

JACKO: What dey for? All yer doing a show or what?

ZIPPY: Show, no man, Ras dis is genuine Ethiopian robes, we is
Rasta man, genuine Rasta man yer do know bout Rastafarian?

JACKO: No, not much.

ZIPPY: Cha me forget you been lock up for long time, well
Rastafarian is black man ting now we discover we identity is
Rastafarian dats it.

JACKO: I hear about it in Jamaica long time.

ZIPPY: Well it a come ter Britain now, we call it Babylon da is Britain
so tell me brother man what it like inside de man place, fer
how long?

JACKO: Five years.

ZIPPY: What is a like?

JACKO: It's not bad, as long as you follow de rules.

ZIPPY: Follow dem rules, me no follow nobody rules.

JACKO: Well when yer inside dere yer have ter or else . . .

ZIPPY: Or else what?

JACKO: Or else, dey make yer pay.

ZIPPY: Cha nobody car make me a do what me do' want ter do.

JACKO: Well inside dey do, a only hope you don't have ter go in.

ZIPPY: Cha me nar go inside dem never catch me, me smarter dem all dem ras.

JACKO: OK.

ZIPPY: But you is a warrior ter ras.

JACKO: How yer mean?

ZIPPY: Sandy she tell we. Sandy tell we how yer en give dem Babylon yer friend en dem names how yer no tell dem notting.

JACKO: Yes.

ZIPPY: Dats heroic ting man, dats what genuine Rasta man go do man.

JACKO: Yes.

ZIPPY: Genuine hero man even Sandy a call yer hero.

JACKO: Tanks, so what you guys do all dey just come here?

ZIPPY: Cha yes is a good place man. Dis is de only place in dis town whey we could come and relax an en get no harassment. We could do we own ting here, an dey en have nobody ter tell we what ter do or asking we what we doing. If we go by the corner, is Panda Car come up, ter ask we questions, Ras clart, dem do' like ter see we doing notting. Everybody must be doing someting, working or going somewhere or coming from somewhere. If dem see people relaxing dem tink dem up ter someting. Dem people do' relax so dem do' like ter see people relax. Dem like have heart attack an give people dem heart attack.

JACKO: Yes.

ZIPPY: Cha brother, me like you me could make you genuine Rasta man.

JACKO: I do' know, I do' know.

ZIPPY: Cha it no sweat you a catch yer spirit.

The Young Graduates
By Victor Rozov; Translated by Miriam Morton

Aleksei, 17; Andrei, 17

Set in former Soviet Russia, *The Young Graduates* defends the right of its young characters to assert their individuality and to make their own decisions concerning the course of their lives. Rozov defends young people's rights to criticize the shortcomings of society, including adults and parents who behave in hypocritical ways. Likewise, the play reinforces the values that make the individual and society spiritually strong and dynamic.

In the scene below, Andrei and his friend Aleksei, both of whom recently graduated from a Moscow 10-year school (an accelerated program), are studying for their college entrance exams.

◆ ◆ ◆ ◆

ANDREI: Don't you feel as though your brains are being twisted?

ALEKSEI: Yes, I do.

ANDREI: (*Slamming his book shut.*) A break – till evening?

ALEKSEI: A break – till evening!

ANDREI: (*Spits on his books.*) You're wasting your time trying to get into that agronomy institute. It only sounds interesting – because they call it an "academy," I suppose. When you are through there they'll put you on a leash and send you to some Godforsaken collective farm. That will bring you mighty little satisfaction.

ALEKSEI: I'm not a beast, to be led off on a leash.

ANDREI: All right, all right, then they'll send you on a train.

ALEKSEI: Then, I'll go.

ANDREI: To improve farm production, I suppose? It's boring as hell out there.

ALEKSEI: Have you ever been in the countryside?

ANDREI: I've heard about it.

ALEKSEI: Moscow is beautiful, but the woods and fields, especially where there's a wide river . . . Did you ever catch fish with a net?

ANDREI: No.

ALEKSEI: Did you ever go spear-fishing at night?

ANDREI: Where do you expect me to have gone spear-fishing? In the Park of Culture and Rest?

ALEKSEI: And did you ever hunt bobcats?

ANDREI: Hunt what?

ALEKSEI: Catch bobcats – alive?

ANDREI: How about you?

ALEKSEI: But you do like ice cream and cake – the easy life?

ANDREI: (*Laughing.*) You're a comedian! Listen, what if I, too, were to apply at your agronomy institute? We'll study together and both of us will pass. You know, it's all the same to me where I go . . .

ALEKSEI: You sure can gab! I've been observing you these two weeks – and I haven't yet decided – whether you're still just a young punk, or already a full-fledged phony.

ANDREI: I can't tell, myself. Probably a mixture of both . . . I'm probably so shallow because everything has been handed to me on a silver platter – the family is well-off . . . they feed and clothe me . . .

ALEKSEI: Is that so? You've found a great excuse for yourself! Afanasy's old man is the captain of a barge fleet on the Enisei River. They also live pretty well – but Afanasy doesn't make excuses for himself the way you do. Katya's dad is a prize-winning author with a good income . . . Listen, brother, don't blame others for your hang-ups. Instead, take a good look at yourself . . . Come, let's go out for some air . . .

ANDREI: Let's wait a while. Galya is coming over soon. We'll all go some place.

ALEKSEI: Why does she hang around you so much?

ANDREI: That should be obvious to you . . .

ALEKSEI: You ought to discourage her.

ANDREI: Why?

ALEKSEI: Because I intend to take her over.

ANDREI: You're so damn sure of yourself . . .

ALEKSEI: It's only fair to warn you . . .

ANDREI: Then I'll also warn Galya.

ALEKSEI: Oh no, you don't! Anyway, what are you – a man or a mouse? (*A pause, then Andrei changes the subject.*)

ANDREI: Listen, Alyosha, what will you say if I do pass my exams after all? Won't you be surprised!

ALEKSEI: Not really. You grasp things quickly. I don't.

ANDREI: Quickly? Not quite – I only master the surface. You get into your studies more deeply. For you it's vital . . .

ALEKSEI: Right now I wish I could do it your way. I'm damn tired!

ANDREI: That's not within one's control. It depends on how a person's brain works.

ALEKSEI: Maybe. I should probably have listened to my mother – and not tried. From a distance everything seemed a lot simpler. Here, when I see how many have come from all over the country for the exams – I often stop and ask myself what chance do I have.

ANDREI: You know, Alyosha, you don't write well. You make lots of mistakes.

ALEKSEI: When I write fast, without thinking, I make fewer mistakes. But when I stop to consider grammatical rules – I'm sure to botch it up.

SCENES
FOR
GROUPS

Mixed Babies
By Oni Faida Lampley

Dena, 16; Reva, 16; Shalanda, 16

Set in the 1970s, Oni Faida Lampley's one-act play *Mixed Babies* concerns a slumber party where five young women contemplate their futures, their role as women, the complexities of race and the ever-looming "Rite of Passage." Within this group we find a diverse set of values, desire, and beliefs. Together these young African-American women attempt to reconcile their place in the world while holding on to their youth and pushing for that which will take them each to womanhood.

The scene below is taken from the second scene in the play entitled, "The Rite of Passage." Here the ritual of becoming a woman, as detailed in an old book of African rites, becomes the new-found attempt to embrace maturity.

Reva enters carrying a thick book, several pieces of old white sheet, some colorful scarves, a bird in a covered cage, and a stainless steel or aluminum soup pot with a few metal and plastic bracelets and necklaces in it, some candles, and matches. Shalanda follows with a ball of string, a knife, tape, and a bottle of sparkling wine. Dena brings up the rear carrying a Wonder Bread bag with a few slices in it, a makeup kit, a Clorox bottle with water in it, and an aerosol can of spray-on glitter.

Reva gives silent directions as to where each set of materials is to be placed. The objects end up forming a circle around the girls.

DENA: Is this going to be like praying?

REVA: No, not really.

SHALANDA: What has this got to do with God?

REVA: Nothing, it's just us and our ancestors –

DENA: Are you an atheist?

REVA: No. (*Pause.*) I'm agnostic . . . I think.

SHALANDA: That's same as atheist.

REVA: No it's not. It means I don't know . . . I think.

SHALANDA: It's the same as saying there is no God!

REVA: No! It's the same as saying I don't know!

DENA: Sssshhhh, y'all! (*Pause.*) I believe in God.

SHALANDA: So do I.

REVA: That's fine with me. I don't care. We just aren't going to say anything about God right now, okay?

DENA: (*To Shalanda.*) Okay?

SHALANDA: Okay.

REVA: Okay. Now –

SHALANDA: He sees everything anyway.

REVA: Maybe it's a she.

DENA: You mean maybe God's a girl?

REVA: Yeah, or a woman.

SHALANDA: I thought you didn't believe in God.

DENA: God ain't no damn woman with periods and everything. If God was a woman the world would really be fucked up. (*Looking up.*) Excuse my french, God . . . Sir.

SHALANDA: (*To Dena.*) You shouldn't talk like that and say "God" in the same sentence!

DENA: Talk like what? I said, "Excuse me." Jesus!

REVA: You all can we just go on please!

SHALANDA: Fine. What do you want me to do?

DENA: (*Laughing.*) God is a woman. Then what's the Holy Trinity, the Supremes? (*Her laughter grows.*) With God in the middle, and Jesus on the right side, and the Holy Ghost –

REVA: That's it! That's it! If y'all aren't going to do this right we are not going to do it at all!

SHALANDA: Sssshhhh!

REVA: Sssshhh my butt! This is a serious serious thing here. We are talking ancestors and blood and stuff like that and if you two can't be serious we just gotta stop now and I don't care if you never get ushered into womanhood! You can just be little girls until you die!

DENA: God! Okay okay okay! What do I gotta do?

REVA: Just be quiet and do what I say.

SHALANDA: We're quiet, okay? Go! What?

DENA: (*Trying to whisper.*) Are we gonna have to sit on the ground? It's kinda wet.

REVA: Yeah. You sit on the ground until I tell you to get up and do something.

DENA: Right, but the ground is wet. Can't we sit on those sheets?

REVA: Uh-uh. The sheets are for wearing in the ritual dance.

SHALANDA: (*Giggling.*) Like ghosts.

DENA: Or the Ku Klux Klan. Lookit. Can't I go inside and get some newspaper or something to sit on? The ground is wet and we're gonna get chiggers!

REVA: Sssshhhh! No! If we keep going in and out the house we'll wake the other girls up and they're gonna wanna know what we're doing.

DENA: So?

REVA: I don't want to even talk to them about it any more. When they see how different we are, they'll be sorry they were scared to try it.

SHALANDA: They weren't scared. They just don't wanna be African.

DENA: I'm not sitting on no wet ground with no chiggers just to be African. They have chairs in Africa, don't they?

REVA: We don't have any now and we can't get any. My mama will wake up! You know she's not gonna let us be outside at four in the morning. Shoot, Dena! Why you have to fuss all the time?

DENA: Me?

REVA: You all stay here and be quiet! Shoot! (*Reva marches into the house. Dena and Shalanda stand quietly for a moment, awkward now that they have to deal with one another. Dena then begins snooping in the piles of stuff they have brought out.*)

DENA: Hey, wow! A knife! (*Pulling it from one of the piles.*) Maybe we're gonna cut ourselves to draw blood or something!

SHALANDA: What? We're gonna what?

DENA: You heard me, we're gonna draw *BLOOOOOOD!!!*

SHALANDA: What? Oh man! I wanted to help Reva and try this and all, but we can't, I mean, I can't, no, uh-huh. There's blood in this? Real blood?

DENA: I don't know Shalanda. Maybe you better go back to bed before the voodoo shit starts and we have you crawling on your belly like a reptile!

SHALANDA: Fuck you Dena –

DENA: Say, "Mother, may I?"

SHALANDA: I'm not gonna be scared. I can do this. You stop picking on me. I don't know why you're here anyway. You always make fun of everything.

DENA: (*Going back to snooping.*) Cuz everything is funny. Besides, I wanna do a "rite of passage." Go home a woman. I'll just go on and be a woman, it's probably easier than this teenage shit. People always telling you what to do, what's wrong with you, what you have to do to get right. You don't know nothing about being picked on, little girl. Shoot, I'm grown already. I got me something special. (*Pause.*) My cousin Richie says I make him feel more like a man than any woman his age ever could. He's off work sometimes when I come home after school. He always wants to do it to me before my mama comes home. He's my friend. All of y'all don't know me. He's my friend. Sometimes he just lies down with me and he falls asleep and he snores. I like that.

SHALANDA: Does it hurt?

DENA: Hell, no. They just tell you that to scare you.

SHALANDA: Do you like it?

DENA: I don't know . . . It's all right. (*Pause.*) Shalanda, don't tell nobody or they might send me away. Okay?

SHALANDA: Okay. (*Peeking under the bird cage cover.*) Hey, there's a real parrot in here! (*Quickly recovers cage, as Dena rushes to look.*)

DENA: Let me see it. (*Peeking.*) Man! I love birds!

SHALANDA: What do you think we're gonna do with a parrakeet?

DENA: I thought you said it was a parrot.

SHALANDA: What's the difference?

DENA: I don't know. (*Peeks a while longer, then recovers the cage.*) Probably kill it. Yep. That's probably what the knife is for. Or maybe we're gonna bite its head off.

SHALANDA: I'm going inside! (*Turns and runs into Reva who's carrying flattened grocery bags.*)

REVA: I got some paper bags. (*Passing a couple grocery bags to each girl.*) You all can sit on these. Now let's get started.

SHALANDA: How're we gonna do this? Listen Reva, I'm not biting off no bird heads or drinking blood or crawling on the ground . . .

REVA: What are you talking about? Dena, stop trying to scare her! That's Serendipity, my Aunt Rose's canary. We're not gonna kill it. It's just here as an animal witness. See, if we were in Africa there'd be nature and real animals all around, but I knew if we wanted an animal, we'd have to bring our own.

DENA: You *got* a dog.

REVA: Yeah, but she might run around or make noise. Serendipity's staying put.

DENA: It might start singing.

REVA: Not covered up. She can't sing in the dark.

SHALANDA: Sorta forgets it's a bird, huh?

DENA: Dumb

REVA: Okay. Now. All the stuff is laid out. Okay. You guys sit on these and face me. (*They comply, with Dena jumping up to get an extra bag. Begins to read/recite.*) "On the coast of West Africa, when the" – oh – hold it! We have to break bread first. Where's the bread?

SHALANDA: Like Holy Communion?

REVA: No, like *Africans.* (*Finds Wonder Bread and passes Dena one slice.*)

DENA: This is all? Here we go, "starving Africans."

REVA: Just break off a piece and pass it to Shalanda.

SHALANDA: I love Wonder Bread. (*Reva reverently leads them through her version of "the breaking of the bread," in silence.*)

REVA: Now. Listen. (*Reads/recites.*) "On the coast of West Africa, when the sun rises on the morning of a young girl's first menses – "

DENA: (*Threatening Shalanda.*) That's BLOOOOD! Blood, bloodbloodbloodblood –

REVA: (*Overriding.*) "It is the dawn of a new day in very way. The news of this (*Carefully, watching Dena.*) "first blood" is sung throughout the community, and all are pleased for her, for soon she will be ready to marry, take a husband to her bed. "Her family begins the preparations for her debut as a maiden, for the moment when she will be presented to the community as one of the young women ready for a full and happy life of bearing and raising children." (*As she reads, she's unsure about how much she likes the "bearing and raising children" part.*)

SHALANDA: I'm gonna be an Olympic swimming coach.

DENA: We know, Bertha Butt!

REVA: "The glorious celebration lasts for one week, during this time her childish girlishness is gently bathed away, and she emerges from the celebration a proud African woman." (*Picks up Clorox bottle.*) Okay, now I bathe each of you.

DENA: Her first!

SHALANDA: She means like baptizing, right?

REVA: Yeah, I'll just do your head.

SHALANDA: But, wait a minute! It'll mess up my hair! My hair'll go back!

DENA: I though it already had!

SHALANDA: I know you shamed! I just got my hair fixed!

REVA: Oh come on! This is the turning point of your entire life and you are worried about your hair napping up?

SHALANDA: Shoot! As much as we pay Mrs. Spencer to do my hair?! My mama will kill me if I go home with beebees all over my head!

DENA: You go to Mrs. Spencer? Shoot, she burns my ears –

REVA: What about you, Dena?

DENA: What about me what?

REVA: Do you want your girlish childishness bathed away?

DENA: Hell, I don't care. Sure. That's not really bleach, is it?

REVA: No.

DENA: Good, I don't wanna be blonde *and* nappy. I'd really be confused then!

REVA: Shalanda, I'll just do your face and hands. You go after
      Dena. Then after I do her, Dena you do me.
DENA: Yas'm. (*Dena stands and bends over, as Reva solemnly pours
      a little water over her head. She shakes and fusses, but steps
      aside for Shalanda. Shalanda takes some water into her
      cupped hands and rubs her face gingerly, then steps aside.
      Dena takes bottle and starts to do Reva but stops.*) Well, first
      you got to take that rag off your head don't you? (*Reva, who
      had forgotten she had it on, reluctantly takes off the scarf,
      exposing a huge, unkempt, thick mass of "unruly" hair.*) Geez-
      zus! You got a lotta hair! Damn! (*Picking at her head.*) What
      all you got in there?
REVA: Just pour! (*Dena floods Reva with rest of water. Reva tries to
      act unperturbed, so the ceremony can continue.*) Sit down,
      please. (*And the girls sit.*)
      "During this time everyone in the community, friends and
      family, lavishes her with gifts – " Let's do Shalanda first. Lavish
      her with gifts, they're over there! (*Dena grabs a handful of
      bracelets, and shoves them at Shalanda. Now their
      movements begin to take on a ritualistic life of their own,
      dreamlike. Perhaps there's music, softly, underneath, as we
      begin to see it actually "happen."*)
      "Bracelets and tiny bells of the finest gold for her arms and
      feet, beautifully translucent cowrie shells for her hair, oils to
      scent and soothe her delicate ebony skin." (*Dena takes up the
      sheets and begins to "dress" Shalanda. At some point,
      perhaps, Reva takes makeup, or dirt, and marks Shalanda's
      cheeks. If this movement is employed, it should be aggressive,
      almost harsh – similar to the ceremonial slap women in some
      societies give their initiates.*)
      "Exquisitely woven garments of dazzling gold and brilliant red
      and peach were draped about her now generously developing
      young body. The mothers of the village, with the elderly
      women leading them, carry her to the river where all the
      impurities and remnants of childhood are washed away, and
      where they tell her the secrets of womanhood." (*Dena stops,*

and stage whispers to Reva.)

DENA: The what?

REVA: (*Side coaching.*) The "secrets of womanhood."

DENA: What are they?

REVA: (*Thinks, then.*) I don't know, make something up, quick.

DENA: (*Tries to remember womanly "secrets" she's been told, then earnestly, in Shalanda's ear.*) Uh – uh –

REVA: (*Prompting.*) "How to care for and cleanse her precious body . . ."

DENA: (*Has an idea.*) Oh, yeah! Wipe from front to back!

REVA: (*This is progress, this is good.*) "How to choose a good man – "

DENA: (*Encouraged.*) Uh – make sure he can drive a stick shift!

REVA: (*On a roll.*) "How to make him happy in the marriage bed – "

DENA: Uh – don't slobber when you sleep!

REVA: "How to control the household finances – "

DENA: Don't tell him how much you make!

REVA: (*Extremely pleased.*) "And how to take time away from her husband and children to replenish herself."

DENA: Don't come home sometimes! (*The "dream" picks up again.*)

REVA: Now you have to state your life intentions. (*The other two girls just look at each other.*) Shalanda, you have to promise the community what kind of woman you will be.

SHALANDA: What should I say, Reva?

REVA: You have to do this part all by yourself. And you have to really really mean it, because you are also promising the ancestors and they don't play. (*Pause.*) Just talk like we're not here.

SHALANDA: I'm Shalanda Breckenridge. I've got twenty letters in my name plus my middle name which is Marie equals twenty-five, so when I'm twenty-five I'm going to get engaged. I might marry Homer Dade, or maybe somebody else. I'll know when I'm twenty-three so we can have a two-year engagement. I like long engagements. I will be an Oceanographer or a Marine Biologist and an Olympic Swimming Coach because I hate being landlocked in stupid Oklahoma City. (But I know I have to lose weight, which I will lose it by Christmas because I'm on a diet, and I really will lose it this time.) P.S. I will also buy my daddy his own filling station so he can work in the daytime on one job just like everybody else. Thank you. (*Pause.*) Amen.

REVA: "She has now joined the circle of women, and will monthly come to the river to be cleansed, soothed, and advised by her sisters. Her delicate skin is – (*Turning page.*) more arid than the Kalahari desert – " what? Wait a minute.
(*Flips back and forth through the pages.*) "Her delicate skin is – "

SHALANDA: (*Frozen in the last position taken.*) What? You said that already.

REVA: It's missing.

DENA: How come it stops there?

REVA: It doesn't but – I can't find the rest of it, it's not here.

DENA: (*Dropping pose.*) Well why the hell did you have us start this if you don't have the whole thing?

REVA: I thought it was here. I mean, this first part was, I assumed it was all here.

SHALANDA: (*Disgusted.*) You should have read the whole thing!

REVA: I mean, but why wouldn't it be here?

DENA: Then where is it?

SHALANDA: This is dumb. It's wet. It's what, four in the morning, I'm wearing a sheet, and you're leaving me dangling with the "secrets of womanhood"!

DENA: Man, I feel stupid!

REVA: We could do me and Dena up to this point.

DENA: Be for real. (*Gathering up her objects.*) Let's go.

REVA: No wait you guys.

SHALANDA: We're finished. Let's go, Reva. (*Kindly.*) Let's go inside.

REVA: But we didn't get to the song part.

DENA: There's music?!

SHALANDA: We did some of it. (*Pause.*) Do you remember the song?

REVA: There wasn't no song. It just said they sing at the end.

SHALANDA: Well . . . (*Pause.*) You wanna sing something?

DENA: Reva, it's almost sunrise and we haven't been to sleep and you don't have the rest of what we're supposed to do. We tried, but . . . (*Pause, then she drops everything, surrendering.*) What do you want to sing?

REVA: An African song.

DENA: Do you know one?

REVA: Umm. "Kumbuya?"

SHALANDA: I hate that song, we sing that, and "We shall Overcome" every doggone Black History Day.

REVA: Is "Yellow Bird" African?

DENA: It's not American. It might be Mexican.

SHALANDA: I think it is African. Sing that, Reva. Then let's go.

REVA: I can't, by myself.

DENA: You start and we'll come in.

REVA: We'll just sing a little of it, so the ancestors know we're serious.

SHALANDA: Right, okay.

REVA: (*Stands a little apart, and slowly begins.*) Yel-low bird up high in banana tree . . . (*Dena stifles a laugh.*) Yel-low bird, you sit all alone like me . . . (*Reva suddenly stops, and says, very simply.*) I can't do this. (*Turns and goes into house.*)

DENA: (*As Reva exits, indicating objects.*) What about all this stuff?

SHALANDA: You made her cry! (*Exits into house.*)

DENA: What? Me? Oh, come on! (*Follows Shalanda abandoning objects onstage. The stage is very quiet for a few seconds, then Reva enters from the house, wiping her eyes. She comes into the yard to collect her things, stacking some objects into the large pot, as the sun is slowly rising. She turns to take the pot into the house. Suddenly we hear chirping. Reva looks around, then continues toward the porch, but the chirping has grown louder. Checking to see if she's being observed, she returns to the bird cage, puts down her pot, squats and listens, without uncovering the cage. Finally, she rises, picking up the pot again, and walks toward the porch. Just before she gets there, she stops, lifts the pot onto her head, squares her*

shoulders, and ascends the porch steps. The lights fade as
Serendipity sings and sings and sings.)

No Saco Nada de la Escuela
By Luis Valdez

Francisco, Monty, Malcolm, Florence, Abraham, Esperanza: all high school students and Teacher, middle age

Luis Valdez's *No saco nada de la escuela* was written as an outgrowth of improvised works by El Teatro Campesino, a farmworker theater, in 1969. One of the leading Chicano playwrights, Valdez's voice is both poetic and astringent. *No saco nada de la escuela* concerns the educational journey of a group of young people from elementary school through college. The students are representative of many races. In the three panels of their story we see the roots of racism develop as very young people and grow into brutal and ugly dimensions by the time the students graduate from college. The play is highly theatrical in style with the characters appearing larger than life.

The scene below forms the second panel of the play and deals with the high school experience.

STUDENTS: (*Backstage, singing.*) Oh hail to thee, our Alma Mater, we'll always hold you dear. (*Then a cheer.*) Rah, rah, sis boom bah! Sock it to them, sock it to them! (*Florence enters stage right. Abraham enters stage left. His neck has a reddish tinge. He tries to hug Florence and is pushed away. He tries again and is pushed away. Florence continues walking.*)

ABRAHAM: Where you going?

FLORENCE: To class.

ABRAHAM: What do you mean to class? I thought we were going steady?

FLORENCE: We were going steady.

ABRAHAM: (*Mimicking her.*) What do you mean "We were going steady?"

FLORENCE: That's right. I saw you walking with that new girl, Esperanza.

ABRAHAM: That Mexican chick? Aw, you know what I want from her. Besides, you're the only girl I love. I'll even get down on my knees for you. (*Falls on knees.*)

FLORENCE: Oh! Abe, don't be ridiculous, get up.

ABRAHAM: (*Getting up.*) Does that mean we're still going steady?

FLORENCE: I guess so.

ABRAHAM: Hot dog! (*From, stage right Francisco enters wearing dark glasses and strutting like a vato loco. Abraham to Florence.*) See that spic over there? Just to show you how much I love you, I'm gonna kick his butt!

FLORENCE: Oh, Abe, you can't be racist!

ABRAHAM: Get out of my way. (*Does warm up exercises like a boxer. Francisco has been watching him all along and has a knife in his hand, hidden behind his back so that it is not visible.*) Heh, greaser, spic!

FRANCISCO: (*Calmly.*) You talking to me, bato?

ABRAHAM: You want some beef? (*Raises his fists.*)

FRANCISCO: (*To audience.*) Este vato quiere pedo. ¿Cómo la ven? ¡Pos que le ponga! (*Pulls out a knife and goes after Abraham.*)

ABRAHAM: (*Backing up.*) Heh, wait a minute! I didn't mean it. I was only fooling. I . . . (*Francisco thrusts the knife toward Abraham. Florence steps in between and stops the knife by holding Francisco's arm. Action freezes. From stage right Malcolm jumps in and struts downstage. He wears a do rag on his head, and sun glasses. He bops around, snapping his fingers; walks up to Francisco and Abraham; looks at knife, feels the blade and walks away as if nothing is happening. From stage right, Monty enters with his arm around Esperanza "Hopi." He runs up to Malcolm.*)

MONTY: Hey, man, what's going on here?

MALCOLM: Say, baby, I don't know. I just don't get into these things. (*Moves away.*)

MONTY: (*Stops him.*) Hey, man, I said what's going on here?

MALCOLM: And I said I don't get into these things! What's the matter with you? Don't you understand? Don't you speak English?

MONTY: (*Angered.*) You think you're better than me, huh? (*Monty grabs Malcolm by the throat, and Malcolm grabs him back. They start choking each other. Teacher enters stage center and observes the fight.*)

MONTY: Nigger!

MALCOLM: Greaser!

MONTY: Spic!

MALCOLM: Coon!

ESPERANZA: Oh, Monty, Monty!

TEACHER: Okay, that's enough. Cut it out, boys! We can settle this
after school in the gym. We might even charge admission.
Everyone to your seats. (*Monty and Malcolm separate.
Francisco puts his knife away and all move back to their seats.*)

TEACHER: Now, before we begin, I want to know who started that
fight.

ABRAHAM: (*Innocently.*) Mr. White? He did, Sir.

FRANCISCO: (*Stands up.*) I didn't start anything. He insulted me!

ABRAHAM: Who you going to believe, him or me? Besides, he pulled
a knife.

TEACHER: (*To Francisco.*) You did what? Get to the Principal's office
immediately!

FRANCISCO: Orale, but you know what? This is the last time I'm
going to the Principal's office for something like this. (*Exits
mumbling.*) Me la vas a pagar, ese, qué te crees.

TEACHER: I don't understand that boy. And he's one of the school's
best athletes. (*Opens mouth, sudden realization. Runs to exit,
shouts after Francisco.*) Don't forget to show up for baseball
practice. The school needs you.

FLORENCE: (*Stands.*) Mr. White? I refuse to sit next to Abraham. He's
a liar!

TEACHER: (*Stands next to Abraham.*) Why, Florence, Abe here is the
son of one of our best grower families.

FLORENCE: Well, I don't care if you believe me or not. But I refuse to
sit next to a liar. (*Gives Abraham his ring.*) And here's your
ring!

TEACHER: All right, sit over here. (*Florence moves across stage and
sits next to Esperanza. Francisco comes strutting in, whistling.*)
I thought I told you to go to the Principal's office.

FRANCISCO: I did, man.

TEACHER: What did he say?

FRANCISCO: He told me not to beat on anymore of his gabachitos. (*Taps Abraham on the head.*)

TEACHER: (*Angered.*) All right, sit over there. (*Indicates a spot beside Florence.*) And you . . . (*To Esperanza.*) over here.

ESPERANZA: (*Stops beside Francisco at center stage.*) You rotten pachuco. (*She sits besides Abraham.*)

FRANCISCO: Uh que la . . .. esta ruca, man (*He sits besides Florence.*)

TEACHER: Now, class, before we begin our high school reports, I'd like to introduce a new student. Her name is Esperanza Espinoza. (*He gives the pronunciation of her name with an Italian inflection.*) It sounds Italian, I know, but I think she's Mexican-American. Isn't that right, dear?

ESPERANZA: (*Self-consciously rising.*) No, my parents were, but I'm Hawaiian. And you can just call me Hopi.

TEACHER: That's fine, Hopi. Now for our high school reports. Florence, you're first.

FLORENCE: (*Drumbeats. Florence walks to center stage, swaying hips like a stripper.*) A is for achievement. Be is for betterment. And C is for (*Bump and grind.*) college! (*More drumbeats as she walks back to her seat.*)

TEACHER: (*Impressed.*) Well! It's good to see that you're thinking of your future. Let's see who's next. Oh yes, Willie.

MALCOLM: (*Hops to his feet.*) I told you, man, my name ain't Willie. It's Malcolm!

TEACHER: All right, you perfectionist! Get up there and give your report.

MALCOLM: (*Struts to center stage. He begins to snap his fingers, setting a rhythm. Everybody joins in.*) A is for Africa. B is for black like me. And C is for community like black ghetto.

ALL: (*Still snapping to rhythm.*) My goodness, Willie, you sure got rhythm. But then after all, all you people do. (*Three final snaps.*)

TEACHER: Now then, Willie, about your report. The first two pages were fine, but that last part about the ghetto . . . don't you think it needs some improvement?

MALCOLM: You're telling me! Don't you think we know it?

TEACHER: Okay, that's a good C minus. Back to your seat. (*Malcolm sits down.*) Abraham, up front!

ABRAHAM: Jabol mein fuehrer! (*Stomps to center stage.*) A is for America: Love or leave it! (*Francisco and Malcolm stand up to leave.*)

TEACHER: Heh, you two! (*Motions for them to sit down.*)

ABRAHAM: B is for better: Better dead than red. And C is for kill, kill, kill! As in the United States Marine Corps. (*Snaps to attention.*)

TEACHER: (*Marches up like a Marine.*) Very good, Abraham!

ABRAHAM: (*Saluting.*) Thank you, sir.

TEACHER: That's an A plus, Abraham!

ABRAHAM: What did you expect, sir?

TEACHER: Dismissed! (*Abraham marches back to seat.*) Monty, up front!

MONTY: Yes, sir! (*Marches sloppily to stage center. Salutes and freezes.*)

TEACHER: (*With contempt.*) Cut that out, and give your report.

MONTY: A is for American. B is for beautiful, like America the Beautiful. And C is for country, like God bless this beautiful American country! Ooooh, I love it. (*He falls to his knees, kisses the floor.*)

TEACHER: (*Grabs Monty by the collar like a dog.*) Here, have a dog biscuit. (*Monty scarfs up imaginary dog biscuit, then is led back to his seat on all floors by Teacher.*) Now, who's next? Oh yes, Hopi.

ESPERANZA: (*Rises prissily, goes to center stage.*) A is for Avon, as in "Ding dong, Avon calling." B is for burgers, which I love, and beans, which I hate! (*Sneers at Francisco.*) And C is for can't as in "I can't speak Spanish." And we have a new Buick Riviera, and my sister goes to the University of California, and we live in a tract home . . .

TEACHER: (*Leading her back to her seat.*) Yes, dear! Just fine!

ESPERANZA: Really, really we do!

TEACHER: I believe you. That deserves a bean . . . uh, I mean B plus. (*Pause.*) Now let's hear from . . . Franky?

FRANCISCO: Yeah, Teach?

TEACHER: What do you mean "yeah, Teach?" You know my name is Mr. White.

FRANCISCO: I know what you name is, ese. But you seem to forget that my name is Francisco, loco.

TEACHER: Get up and give your report, you hoodlum.

FRANCISCO: Orale, ese vato, llévatela suave. (*Moves to center stage.*) A is for amor, como amor de mi raza.

TEACHER: What!

FRANCISCO: B is for barrio como where the raza lives. (*Teacher growls.*) And C is for carnalismo.

TEACHER: (*Heated.*) How many times have I told you about speaking Spanish in my classroom?! Now what did you say?

FRANCISCO: Carnalismo.

TEACHER: (*At the limit of his patience.*) And what does that mean?

FRANCISCO: Brotherhood.

TEACHER: (*Blows up.*) Get out!!

FRANCISCO: Why? I was only speaking my language. I'm a Chicano, ¿que no?

TEACHER: Because I don't understand you, and the rest of the class doesn't understand you.

FRANCISCO: So what? When I was small, I didn't understand English, and you kept flunking me and flunking me instead of teaching me.

TEACHER: You are permanently expelled from this high school!

FRANCISCO: Big deal! You call yourself a teacher! I can communicate in two languages. You can only communicate in one. Who's the teacher, Teach? (*Starts to exit.*)

MONTY: We're not all like that, teacher.

FRANCISCO: ¡Tú te me callas! (*Pushes Monty aside and exits.*)

TEACHER: That's the last straw! A is for attention. B is for brats like that. And C is for cut out. High school is dismissed! (*Teacher exits, taking high school sign with him. Malcolm exits also at opposite side of stage. Abraham, Florence, Esperanza and Monty rise, facing each other.*)

MONTY: (*Looking at Florence.*) Oh, Hopi?

ESPERANZA: (*Looking at Abraham.*) Yes?

ABRAHAM: (*Looking at Esperanza.*) Oh, Flo?

FLORENCE: (*Looking at Monty.*) Yeah?

ABRAHAM AND MONTY: (*Together.*) Do you wanna break up?

FLORENCE AND ESPERANZA: (*Together.*) Yeah! (*Monty takes Florence by the arm; Abraham takes Esperanza.*)

MONTY: Oh boy, let's go to a party.

ABRAHAM: Let's go to a fiesta. (*All exit.*)

Shakin' The Mess Outta Misery
By Shay Youngblood

Daughter, young woman; Miss Lamama, middle-aged, and Miss Shine, middle-aged

Shay Youngblood's *Shakin' The Mess Outta Misery* is set in a small southern town and moves through time between the 1920s and the present. Ms. Youngblood describes the setting as "a place where memories and dreams coincide." The story concerns Daughter, a young black woman orphaned at an early age and raised by a number of loving black women. When the play begins, Daughter, now in her late twenties, has returned to her hometown for the funeral of the last of the women who raised her. Daughter serves as the play's narrator as well as playing herself as a child through the delicate story of the young woman's coming of age. The richness of Daughter's present-day life is due to the caring imprint each of the women of her youth made on her journey to womanhood. The play mixes events and stories from the past in a theatrical, almost ritualistic, presentation that offers a unique perspective on the role of black women during this century.

In the scene below, Miss Lamama, with Daughter's help, reenacts a story from the past.

Daughter on stage. Miss Lamama enters and mimes hanging clothes on the line.

DAUGHTER: As time got closer for me to go to the river, I started spending more time alone with my Big Mamas, women who gave stories as gifts. Miss Lamama was special in that. Being married to an African, Miss Lamama learned their tradition of storytelling. She wore pink slippers everyday but Sunday when she sang in the choir. I loved hearing her catch notes with her voice and then letting them fly over our heads into the congregation like birds. When Miss Lamama was telling a story her voice was like that too.

MISS LAMAMA: Now, Daughter, I'm gonna tell you about the time Miss Shine got even for a four hundred-year-old wrong, as it was told to me. And 'long as I'm black I'll never forget it. (*Miss Shine enters and mimes rolling in tea cart.*) Miss Shine lived down the street from us. She had worked in the governor's mansion ever since her husband died and left her with no insurance and a lot of bills to pay. But Miss Shine caught on quick that the governor and his wife was just simply country crackers. The funniest thing she had to do was pour tea every day at four o'clock for the governor and his wife. They would sit there in the living room, quiet as two rocks in a river, slurping that sweet tea till suppertime. This particular December, our colored high school chorus was selected to sing at the governor's mansion on Christmas Eve. For weeks that's all folks talked about.

MISS SHINE: You know I'm gonna be there to see our children show out. The governor done asked me already to stay past sundown on Christmas Eve.

MISS LAMAMA: Weeks before the first Christmas pine was chopped, Miss Shine was busy polishing cabinets full of silver and starching closets full of linen. Her biggest job, and one she loved best and saved for last, was cleaning the grand French crystal chandelier that hung in the entry hall to the mansion.

MISS SHINE: It gimme time to think.

MISS LAMAMA: Two days before the singing a strong feeling came over Miss Shine like something bad was about to happen. But, Christmas Eve when she seen them three yellow school buses roll around the circle driveway, Miss Shine's heart was near 'bout busting with joy. She knowed we were gonna do her proud that night. Them little white children was dressed up in blue jackets for the boys and blue skirts for the girls. But we had on long white robes with gold sashes over our shoulders looking just like black angels. The first group of them little white children sang they Christmas carols in high-pitched cut-off notes that didn't sound right to Miss Shine, but she clapped when they was done. The second group wasn't much better, but, Lord, then them colored children broke loose. I led the choir. When we was done there was a deep hush, quiet like even God had stopped what *she* was doing to listen. Then they sent for the children to come inside for hot chocolate. But that governor only invited them white children inside for hot chocolate. Our faces went soft and sad like they was

gonna cry. Except for Corine. Her face was hard like she
wanted to throw a brick through that mansion window. Your
Big Mama looked like she didn't 'spect no less. Shine looked
at us, something inside of her broke in two.

MISS SHINE: She was madder than a foam-mouth dog. But what
could she do? She left it in the Lord's hands, and He came
through. With no warning. the big, round crystal that hung
from the middle of the chandelier fell with a loud crash on the
marble floor, breaking into a million pieces. It didn't hurt
nobody, but Shine took it to be a sign.

MISS LAMAMA: Miss Emmie seen Shine staring and snapped up
"Shine, get a broom and sweep up this mess before one of
the children gets hurt."

MISS SHINE: She swept up every piece of crystal she could find. They
sparkled like diamonds, but every jagged edge was a dagger
in her heart. Folks say things changed, but it's still like slavery
times, Miss Shine's mind eased back, way, way back. She
heard a chant far off and deep as slave graves and old Africa.

MISS LAMAMA: (*Beats her calabash in time.*) Blood, boil thick, run
red like a river, slave scream, wail, moan after they dead.
Daddy lynched, Mama raped, baby sister sold down river.
Slaves scream, wail, moan after they dead. The cook knew
what to do to save the race, stop the screams.

MISS SHINE: Miss Shine all of a sudden knowed what she had to do
to save the race. She was possessed by her power. When she
got home she went into her bedroom and she got the wood
bowl her mama give her and the iron head of her husband's
hammer. She come back to the table spread with all the broke
crystal and ground it till sweat dripped off her face into the
bowl. And she ground it, and she ground it and she ground it
till it was fine as dust. Then she tied it in a corner of her slip.
When Miss Shine has to go back to work after New Year's she
was ready, almost happy to go.

MISS LAMAMA: Miss Emmie stopped her from washing the lunch
dishes to tell her, "Shine, we ready for tea." Miss Shine yes
ma'amed her, looking direct in her eyes. Miss Emmie wasn't

used to colored making eye contact and she near 'bout run out the kitchen. Miss Shine went on as usual fixing tea. She put the kettle on to boil.

DAUGHTER AND MISS LAMAMA: Blood boil thick.

MISS LAMAMA: She kept hearing whispers. She poured the boiling water over the tea leaves and strained it into the big silver teapot.

DAUGHTER AND MISS LAMAMA: Run red like a raging river.

MISS LAMAMA: She took down two china cups with a flower pattern and set 'em straight on matching saucers.

DAUGHTER AND MISS LAMAMA: Nobody know how the master get sick.

MISS LAMAMA: Miss Shine put everything on the big tea cart.

DAUGHTER AND MISS LAMAMA: Nobody know how he die.

MISS LAMAMA: She untied the knot in the corner of her slip and emptied the fine crystals into the sugar bowl and . . .

DAUGHTER AND MISS LAMAMA: Stirred it up, stirred it up, stirred it up goooood. (*Sighs of relief.*)

MISS LAMAMA: Miss Shine kept pouring tea for the governor and Miss Emmie for more than two weeks before she disappeared. Some folks say she moved to an entirely colored town in Texas, other folks say she wasn't really of this world in the first place. Nobody ever see Miss Shine again. From then on, the colored high school chorus started singing Christmas carols at the colored nursing home every year to honor our own folks. Nobody ever talking about wanting to sing for the governor no more. Every time I sing "Spirit of the Living God" solo, I dedicate it to Miss Shine, wherever she is. Daughter, remember, you must always honor your ancestors.

DAUGHTER: Yes ma'am. There are all kinds of gifts you can give and receive, Miss Lamama's was pride.
(*Miss Lamama exits singing line from mournful gospel.*)

12-1-A
By Wakako Yamauchi

Harry, 25; Koko, 17; Ken, 19

The title of Wakako Yamauchi's moving play represents the symbols for the living
quarters in a Japanese incarceration camp in Poston, Arizona, 1942: block 12, barrack 1,
unit A. This is the setting for the play that concerns the Tanaka family, American citizens
incarcerated in this camp because they are Japanese, during a time when the United
States was at war with Japan. Uprooted from their home, dropped into a squalid
environment, the Tanakas grapple to preserve their dignity and survive while at the same
time the young people attempt to sort out their role in a bleak future. No one knows
when the imprisonment will end, if ever. The play has a particularly stinging truth when
one realizes that Ms. Yamauchi was, herself, interned in just such a camp during World
War II.

In the scene below, Koko, the Tanaka's daughter, encounters Ken and Harry in the
barracks. Koko and her brother, Mitch, knew Ken from high school. Harry, who is
retarded, is protected by Ken.

HARRY: (*Setting down his hand.*) Gin!
KOKO: (*Checking his hand.*) No, Harry. Every trick has to have at
    least three cards. See, you have only two here. (*Shows him her
    hand.*) You have to have three cards of the same suit.
HARRY: Oh yeah. I forgot.
KOKO: We'll play something else. How about . . .
HARRY: I don' wanta play cards.
KOKO: Okay. Well . . . you want me to read to you?
HARRY: I can read. (*Spins his hat.*)
KOKO: You want to talk?
HARRY: Okay.
KOKO: Well . . . Tell me about your mother.
HARRY: She's dead.
KOKO: Well, shall we talk about your father, then? What's your
    father like? Is he . . . (*Harry moves from the table to the
    upstage bench.*) Is he tall? Is he short? Is he . . .
HARRY: He's not very nice.

KOKO: How come? Does he hit you?

HARRY: He don' talk to me.

KOKO: No, that's not very nice.

HARRY: He always say, "Baka, baka . . . " Baka means stupid. Make me feel bad. He don' like me.

KOKO: Harry. He likes you. He's like my mom. She keeps nagging, "Find a job, go to work, find a nice man." Sometimes I think just because she tells me to, I won't. Funny, hunh? (*Harry Laughs.*) I don't know why I feel so . . . I don't know. Maybe it's the weather. It's so hot here. Maybe it's this place. Maybe it's the world . . . the war.

HARRY: Yeah . . .

KOKO: Maybe everyone feels like this. This place is like . . . like a vacuum . . . You're shut out from the outside and inside everyone pretends like nothing's wrong.

HARRY: Yeah.

KOKO: Like this is normal. But it's not normal. What are people really feeling?

HARRY: I don't know.

KOKO: Maybe we shouldn't worry about things we have no power to change. Maybe we should go to work every day, smile hello, say good-bye . . . spread small joys . . . inflict little hurts . . . skirt around this whole crazy situation. Maybe this is the way it's supposed to be.

HARRY: (*Depressed.*) Yeah . . .

KOKO: (*Realizing she's depressing Harry.*) Yo's got another job. She's so strong . . . all alone here. I'd probably fall apart. But, of course, I have my mom and Mitch . . .

HARRY: Yeah . . .

KOKO: And Yo and Ken . . .

HARRY: And me, too.

KOKO: Harry?

HARRY: Hunh?

KOKO: Do you . . . do you think he likes me?

HARRY: Who?

KOKO: You know who. (*Harry shrugs and turns inward.*) I suppose

I'd know it if he did . . . wouldn't have to ask anyone.
(*Ken enters and peeks through the door. Koko is surprised and embarrassed.*)

KEN: Hi!

KOKO: Oh! Hi! Ah . . . aren't you working today?

KEN: I'm out in the field today. Hot enough for you? Hi, Harry.
(*Enters and sits at the table with them.*)

KOKO: What a cushy job. What do you do?

KEN: Oh . . . I just . . . I just walk around. See what's going on. (*Ken holds out a candy bar for Koko. He gives Harry the one he brought for himself.*) And for Harry. They're selling them at the canteen today.

KOKO: (*Her eyes grow wide.*) Candy bar! I haven't had one of these since . . . I'll save mine for later. (*Breaks the bar in half and gives one half back to Ken.*)

HARRY: (*Overlaps.*) Thanks. (*Eats carefully.*)

KEN: (*To Koko.*) Eat it now. Otherwise it'll melt.

Welcome Home Jacko
By Mustapha Matura

Zippy, Marcus, Dole, and Fret, all 17-21

Mustapha Matura, perhaps the leading dramatist of West Indian origin, wrote *Welcome Home Jacko* after visiting a community youth center in Sheffield, England. The center was a place for young people to socialize apart from the pangs of social oppression and racism. The play, set in just such a center, concerns a group of young people struggling for a Black identity. As the four young West Indians interact in the Club, exploring their place in the world, they assert their beliefs. Sandy, the white girl who manages the club, is preparing to welcome home Jacko, who has spent the last five years in prison for raping a girl.

The scene below between the four young men opens the play.

A bar counter on the side with stools, also table and chairs against the wall. Posters of Africa, Ethiopia, Haile Selassie, Youth Employment, a Police PR poster. Across the ceiling a larger banner saying: WELCOME HOME JACKO. The rear stairs leading to an office upstairs. In the corner a Juke Box-Football machine. The four young men are playing a football machine.

ZIPPY: Ras Clart me beat yer.

MARCUS: Bet what you a miss ter Ras Clart, you a hit one ball you a call dat beat.

ZIPPY: Aright, make we play one more game, Dole yer ready?

DOLE: Me no want te play no mor Man, him a make ter much Ras Clart noise make we play some Dominoes.

ZIPPY: Cha Man, I we play.

MARCUS: Me an Fret go clart yer ras, eh Fret?

FRET: Yea, yea, make we play, en last round, first five win.

MARCUS: Wha yer say?

ZIPPY: Me ready Dole.

DOLE: Aright, make we play, him a make ter much noise make we shut him Ras Clart mouth.

MARCUS: Wait, wait, wha we a play for?

ZIPPY: Wha him mean?

MARCUS: Coke, make we play fer Coke, who a lose him have ter buy, wha yer a say?

ZIPPY: Cha why not you no win.

DOLE: Yea.

MARCUS: Make we see.

ZIPPY: Aright

(*They play. Zippy and Dole, Marcus and Fret.*)

ZIPPY: Move dey, yer Ras shift, eh.

DOLE: Block him Ras.

MARCUS: Go way Block yer Bomba, dat . . . go in, go in.

ZIPPY: Block him Cha.

MARCUS: Move Fret, block im Fret.

ZIPPY: Goal.

MARCUS: Cha Fret you a let de Ras Clart Man score him a get easy goal, me no why him a score me no had me sounds wit me punch me a dub, Fret.

FRET: Him a lucky, him a lucky.

(*Goes, punches Juke Box (Reggae). Throughout the later games music is played.*)

ZIPPY: Lucky me Ras Clart dat a skill, skill from above, skill from Jah.

MARCUS: Jah, me Ras, wha you no bout Jah, dat a luck.

ZIPPY: Me no Jah, me talk ter Jah, him talk ter me, me an him communicate him a tell me hit de Ras Clart ball square, me hit it square it a go in square.

MARCUS: Cha.

ZIPPY: Me an Dole, we hand guided wha yer say Dole?

DOLE: Cha, him a seek him revenge.

MARCUS: Him a right me a hit yer Ras wid de Rod a Correction come Fret, block him Ras.

(*They play.*)

DOLE: Go way, go way yer Ras.

ZIPPY: Block him, block him Ras Clart.

MARCUS: Go in, go in, go, go.

ZIPPY: Block in, cha him gone.

MARCUS: Block him break Fret, Fret, block him, cross.

FRET: We have him de Fret ter Ras.

MARCUS: Good him Ras worry now, go in, go in.

ZIPPY: Dole.

MARCUS: Goal, goal ter Ras.

ZIPPY: Dole you let de Ras Clart Man jinx yer.

MARCUS: Whey yer communicate wid Jah gone me just cut yer wires. Jah do' want ter know you, him a have better Ras Clart ting ter do.

ZIPPY: Aright one all.

MARCUS: Dat goal was scored by de Lion of Judea, de warrior of Redemption ter Ras Clart, me no me should have me dub.

ZIPPY: Make we play. Make we play.

MARCUS: Fret like him in a hurry ter buy Coke, him feeling rich come, Resurrection is at hand all Hypocrites I will shed blood come to Canaan.

(They play.)

ZIPPY: Block him Ras.

DOLE: Me block im.

ZIPPY: Up, up.

MARCUS: Me have it, me have it.

ZIPPY: Have me Ras, dey.

MARCUS: Me have it.

ZIPPY: Take him Dole.

DOLE: Me have im, him gone.

MARCUS: Fret him coming.

FRET: Me have im.

ZIPPY: Have dat yer Ras.

MARCUS: Fret.

ZIPPY: Goal, goal, fer Ras.

MARCUS: Cha Fret you let de Man walk round yer.

FRET: Me stop him.

MARCUS: Him score Man.

ZIPPY: Two one, yer see Jah will guide him servant to Paradise him will guide him Warrior ter wreck vengeance on dose who face Judgment, de Sword of Jah is sharp and swift, wit love on one side and blood on de odder.

MARCUS: Judgment me Ras we have two more ter come we a go
　　see who have Judgment.

ZIPPY: Righteousness is mine to give said Jah, you a get him
　　punishment him wrath.

MARCUS: Shut yer Bomba.

DOLE: Make we play him, don't believe him have ter see yer him ter
　　believe, him a unbeliever, him one a dem who have ter feel
　　him pain.

　　(*They play.*)

MARCUS: Watch im Fret.

FRET: Me see im.

ZIPPY: See, im, yer could see Lightning yer could see de Desert
　　Wind, see dat.

MARCUS: Good Fret.

FRET: Me see him Ras me read him like Genesis, Chapter One.

ZIPPY: Block him Dole.

MARCUS: Judgment come to him deserving.

DOLE: Me have him.

MARCUS: Have Ras.

ZIPPY: Watch im Dole, him wait.

DOLE: Me have im Ras covered.

MARCUS: Cover dat yer Heathen.

DOLE: Me have im.

MARCUS: Cover dat yer Hypocrite.

DOLE: Me cover im.

MARCUS: Cover dat yer Pagan.

DOLE: Me . . .

MARCUS: Goal, goal.

ZIPPY: Dole, him . . .

MARCUS: Him what him cover dats what him do, him conquer all
　　Jericho is dats what him do, eh Fret?

FRET: Cha.

MARCUS: Make we show one unbelievers who take de road ter
　　greed an vanity dat rudeness do' pay, Cha me could taste de
　　Ras Clart Coke already.

ZIPPY: Last game, two all.

DOLE: Him a make himself, Ras lose make him see.

MARCUS: Me a want one large glass ter Ras Clart, wid big ice an a straw, eh Fret?

FRET: Cha, dem a miss, dem goal.

ZIPPY: Aright make we see. (*They play.*) Watch im Dole.

DOLE: Me have him.

MARCUS: Have . . . Fret him come.

FRET: Me have him.

ZIPPY: Have Bomba, him come Dole.

MARCUS: Dole a sleep ter Ras, me a shepherd.

FRET: Me a once walk round him.

DOLE: Me have him.

ZIPPY: Him a want ter sneak in, like Judas.

MARCUS: Judas me Ras, me a son of Jah, yer Hypocrite, take im Fret.

FRET: Me have im Ras.

ZIPPY: Have dat yer Ras.

FRET: Me tell yer me have him him path block im power miss.

MARCUS: Give him Judgment ter Ras.

ZIPPY: Dole im . . .

MARCUS: Judgment come.

ZIPPY: Him try Dole, block him.

MARCUS: Goal, goal, in yer Ras Clart, yer Bomba Clart, yer tink yer could escape de Sword of Correction you Hypocrite, Jah a say all will succumb, an him word is law.

ZIPPY: Dole you let dis Ras Clart beat we, Cha.

DOLE: Him lucky, Man.

MARCUS: Me no beat yer me righteousness beat yer, Cha Fret, dem a Ras Clart, en know de Warriors of Haile Selassie de Lion of Judah, de Lord of Lords de King of Kings, wen dem see him. (*He beats his chest.*)

FRET: Whey de Coke dem, me a tirsty, all yer a deal Coke.

MARCUS: Cha yea, me a hot too, me a want me nice cool down make me gather me wisdom, ter confront dem Hypocrites, get dem Cokes.

ZIPPY: Make we wait till Sandy a come.

MARCUS: De Coke behind de Bar Man.

ZIPPY: Sandy have de keys Man.

MARCUS: Cha go behind de Bar and break him Ras, Man, me want me Coke.

ZIPPY: Nar man.

MARCUS: Whey Sandy?

ZIPPY: She upstairs in de office.

MARCUS: Well call she down ter Ras, like yer want me break de Ras Clart lock or yer do' want ter pay fer yer sins.

ZIPPY: Me a pay, me a pay, Dole give Sandy a call.

DOLE: Cha make dem call, she na drink dem, Jah say, 'Make men toil fer him rewards,' me do' like asking she Ras fer notting.

ZIPPY: Call de Ras Clart woman nar.

MARCUS: Cha me go call she nar fraid no Hypocrite me power stronger dan dem.

Permission Acknowledgments